Ready or Not

Children, spirituality and journeying together

Ready or Not

Children, spirituality and journeying together

Ruth Harvey

wild goose publications

www.**ionabooks**.com

Poems, prose, readings © the individual contributors
Compilation © 2012 Ruth Harvey
First published 2012 by
Wild Goose Publications, Fourth Floor, Savoy House,
140 Sauchiehall Street, Glasgow G2 3DH, UK,
the publishing division of the Iona Community. Scottish Charity No. SC003794.
Limited Company Reg. No. SC096243.

ISBN 978-1-84952-217-5

Cover design © 2012 Wild Goose Publications
Cover photograph © David Coleman

The publishers gratefully acknowledge the support of the Drummond Trust,
3 Pitt Terrace, Stirling FK8 2EY in producing this book.

Overseas distribution
Australia: Willow Connection Pty Ltd, Unit 4A, 3–9 Kenneth Road, Manly Vale,
NSW 2093
New Zealand: Pleroma, Higginson Street, Otane 4170, Central Hawkes Bay
Canada: Bayard Distribution, 10 Lower Spadina Ave., Suite 400, Toronto,
Ontario M5V 2Z

Printed by Bell & Bain, Thornliebank, Glasgow

Contents

III. Made in God's Image   61

IV. Wide Compassion   83

Introduction

The story of this book

We are all God's children. As a child I relished this truth in the (at that point unarticulated) knowledge that I truly belonged to the whole inhabited earth, the *oikoumene* of God's kingdom. But no such grand notions could prepare me for what it actually felt like, in 1999, to be pregnant and full of the fears and the hopes of one carrying an unborn baby. I was ravenous – for good, wholesome food to fill my growing belly. But I was ravenous in another way too. I found not only that I craved three full breakfasts daily, but that I was hungry for reflections to feed me, body, mind and spirit through gestation. And so I searched for material that wove my spiritual yearnings with my physical and emotional path.

I found poems about pregnancy and motherhood, essays and narratives about the ups and downs of parenting, novels and theological reflections on the nature of motherhood. It was good material. But I was hungry for more. My senses and hunger had been alerted to children in a new way through my own pregnancy. My questions continued to grow as did my belly and the children of our home. What could children teach me about God, about faith, about the spiritual journey that, somewhere along the path of growing up, I had momentarily lost? In what ways did I need to open my ears and my heart to the still small voice of God talking to me through the unaccountably beautiful (at 3am?!) not so still small voice of the child in my arms?

If we are all children of God, if God dwells within each one of us, for all time, then in what ways could I retune my active mind to the wisdom of the children within and in my life?

And in the meantime, as life continued to grow chaotically and beautifully around us in our home, as I sat with my own needs and longings, we imperceptibly collected what turned out to be a notebook of original, deeply moving or funny things that our children began to say. Just writing down, word for word, some of their pearls of wisdom took on a life of its own, and reminded me that children live and breathe and voice a depth of wisdom about God.

So the questions continued to grow and deepen, as I reflected as carefully as I could on the spiritual insights and wisdom coming from our very own children.

Conversations with friends about living alongside children, and the impact they have on our own spiritual journeying continued to deepen. I realised that there are few neat categories or essay collections that can capture the breadth and depth, the joy and the sorrow of being around children. But the desire to capture some of this 'rainbow story' grew, as the focus shifted from stories about birth and childhood, to those about the impact of children on our own adult spiritual journeys. And the question crystallised:

'In what ways has being around children, whether as their parent or godparent, their aunt or uncle, grandparent, adoptive parent, foster-sibling or companion, deepened and broadened your own spiritual path?'

I have been involved with the Iona Community all of my life, and have been a member since 1994. And so I began to share this question with friends and relations within the Community, who have shared in so many ways their growing journey of faith with me. I shared this question too with friends and colleagues from outside the Iona Community – and so the responses – and the collection – began to grow.

Each year since, more contributions have been offered spontaneously or have been coaxed out after a particularly inspiring conversation. What is here, therefore, is not complete, or finished. Not polished or perfect. It is a collection offered at this particular point in time, exploring the organic glory of faith shared, and made wholly 'perfect' through our encounter with children and young people.

These pieces, written over a period of 10 years, capture a moment, or a thought, or an experience in the flow of life. Life moves on. Children grow. Stories deepen. In the midst of such flux, my hope is that the timeless wisdom gleaned through living alongside children remains.

Revisiting my childhood

Being amongst children is not a completely new experience for any of us, who have grown up with siblings, or cousins, with neighbours or peers. For my part, with brothers and a sister, foster siblings, nieces and nephews, the children of friends, godchildren, and now my own daughters, it feels like I have been 'accompanying' children all my life. My own childhood, lived for the first ten years in intentional Christian communities, in Glasgow with the Gorbals Group, and then on Iona as part of the Iona Community, had been a mixture of immersion amongst many families for short periods, with long-term connection to a tiny group of children in an island school.

At the same time I had in part experienced being collectively parented. So what did the other adults in my life, some parents, some not, have to say about the impact of children on their own spiritual journeys, particularly in an intentionally spiritual context? Many of the offerings here interweave actual experiences of being parented, along with reflections on what it means to be a parent, side by side with moving encounters with young children in our own adult lives. These pieces are autobiographical in the best sense of that word: reflective, insightful, humorous and deeply personal while at the same time revealing universal truths. Neat categories continue to evade.

Ordering the pieces

As the collection gathered, the question remained: how to present these unique stories in one cohesive volume? Should the contributions simply appear in the order received; should they follow a chronology based on the pattern of birth, living, death; or should they 'talk' to each other in a wholly subjective pattern?

In the end the questions became too vast, and the possibilities endless. While through this collection there is a consciously woven thread binding the stories one to the other in a light-touch pattern which makes sense to me, it is for the reader to engage with each piece separately, allowing one to speak to the other, and to the reader's own story. And thus the invitation remains open: in what ways, for you, does being in the company of children deepen and broaden your own spiritual path?

Thanks

My thanks go to Neil Paynter, Sandra Kramer and the Wild Goose Publications team whose patience and professionalism have steered this book to birth. Thank you in particular to Suzanne Swanson whose poem gave a title to this book. 'Ready or not, here we come …' could be an anthem for children everywhere. My heartfelt thanks to each of the authors, who contributed stories from the heart; and to the children and young people who inspired them; and in particular to Maeve, Freya and Sophie, and of course to Nick: thank you for your wisdom, your humour and your creativity.

Ruth Harvey

Ready or not

There's a prayer
in here, a prayer

to God the father
and the mother, God

the child, God the arms
and the breast, this

prayer: keep us
in all our desire and lack.

Our failings
are not our whole.

You know us. Carry us
as we have carried within

our children. Listen
as we are learning to listen

to deep life in small bodies new
to the world and full

of refusal to use
our glazed eye. Follow

the skips and stumbles
of our feet following

the feet and the mouths
and the beating of heart

laid to heart, bass
and treble, rhythm and melody

trading anchor and flight.
Oh, the spirit that can enter

when the wind of God
blows the breath

of a child through our
bodies ready

or not.
Keep us.

Suzanne Swanson

Arriving and Departing ...

... On how children take us literally and metaphorically full circle to the liminal spaces of life, to those edges where we encounter beginnings and endings, arriving and departing, life and death ...

Heartbeat

The still small voice,
pat, pat, pat.
The divine spark,
phut, phut, phut.
From the depths, from the dark,
present, here, there, within.
Thump. Thump. Thump.

No sign, no bump, no light,
no visible form.
This is the voice of the spirit,
this is the sound of the soul,
this is the accent of the unborn,
born within.

Ruth Harvey

Full circle

The extraordinary thing about conception is the intimacy between life and death. After the pain and desolation of an early miscarriage I learned how often the micro-cells of a life are seemingly tossed aside by a body – how often this most longed-for moment is held in suspension, only to be discarded. Yet no matter how 'routine' it may be, the agony of a miscarriage, of a death can be numbing and is often lived through in silence.

In the Western northern culture which I inhabit we are sometimes encouraged to hold the knowledge of a pregnancy 'secret' until the first trimester is over: until we are more confident that the baby will live. And yet it was at this very time, when the risk of miscarriage was greatest, when I was most vulnerable – feeling 'blooming awful', grim with the 'joys' of morning sickness – that I felt I most needed my friends. And if we were to lose our baby, then surely that was the time we most needed to lean on others. Certainly for me this turned out to be the case. So for each subsequent pregnancy I made sure I had a strong team of friends around me from the earliest days, there to support me and to listen, if I should lose the baby again.

The fragility of my second pregnancy was terribly poignant, therefore, and no more so than when I found myself in Linton churchyard in 1999. Taking part in a retreat, I took myself off to a quiet spot – then looked up and realised, of course, that, as I hadn't gone out of the gate, I was still in the churchyard, surrounded by gravestones. My thoughts turned from the solid slabs of stone surrounding me, each one summarising a life in dates and names, to the fragile cells frantically at work weaving life deep in the darkness of my womb.

The following poem reflects some of my thoughts on that July morning:

A poem to an unborn child

In this place death
and life commingle –
names and dates written on stone
scribe the moment of life,
    the moment of death;
name the living and the dead.

The soft spiky touch of
the yew-tree roots me here,
in this place –
grounds me
on this earth –
firmly keeps me,
holds, pushes me
forward into the paradox
of living and dying.

In your place,
the dark, hidden, warming
womb within,
life and death commingle.
The spark of creation has been born,
in love, passion, flesh of our flesh,
    seed of our seed,
    bone of our fragile bone.
The sparkle of the soul now lives,
God-filled, Spirit-pregnant, holding, keeping,
warming, pushing out into the paradox
of a world of living and of dying.

Your vulnerable world
is close to truth
lives near to light
in the extreme darkness,
is held and nurtured
in the certainty of life beyond life.

Your fragile world
lives close to death,
to an ending that has no logic,
is clothed in mystery.

In my hand,
a rock – firm yet light,
solid, sure,
aged beyond belief.

In the paradox of life with death
in this place, and in your place,
let this rock be a reminder
of the solid, moving ground
of love in the midst of mystery.

Ruth Harvey

Birthing

I have given birth four times. Doubtless there are very many activities I am more practised at. Yet birthing is something I have always felt at home doing, and perhaps that is because it is such an inward-outward movement.

As a psychologist, my work is often focused on attending to what is happening in the unseen places of people's lives – the places where they feel or think or hold opinions. This might seem like an inward focus, yet it is in fact usually a process of connecting with the unsaid or unnoticed aspects of the person or family or group in order that there can be a movement towards an overt way of being which is more useful, authentic or powerful for the person or people concerned. This process is of course always most interested in the marginalised story or the exceptional voice, often the most silent and least powerful, because it is this hidden treasure which, when brought to light, can be the most dynamic agent of change.

Yes, looking inwards on its own is not what happens when we do this work. Moving outwards to new life is actually what occurs. And this is why it reminds me of birth. Or perhaps why birth was so familiar to me. Because birth cannot happen powerfully and naturally unless you move in and out. The inward movement is into your body, your instinctive urges, your sacred womanhood. You have to move to the limen – the threshold – the vulnerable place where you surrender all. All that has been – your desires for the future, your intellectual fantasy of control – all these must be left at the door to the threshold of birthing. And here in this zone, you go in, deep into yourself, to the place where only you and God can go, to the source, to the hub, to the waters of death and birth.

And of course when you are inside the limen there is a great rush of power which is the energy of the birthing, and there is an overwhelming series of waves of pain, which are the moments of surrender to the new life, and there are the pauses, the spaces in which to resurface before the waves take you forward again. When you are deep within yourself, powerful and free, in complete submission to the process, very little can interfere with the birthing. It is like being utterly hooked up to God: terrifying and amazing and costly and the most positive act of self-giving going.

And of course it all ends with the movement out, from one of the most marginalised and silenced parts of the human body, into a world very keen to idolise an infant's story of innocence and hope. Into a world where our national laws may mean that a mother with a life-limiting illness must return to a country where there is virtually no treatment, leaving her child behind in care or taking him with her to be orphaned. Into a world where violence is commonplace in the home, legal and illegal drugs are standard ways of coping with emotion, and poverty of self-respect accompanies the struggle with housing and benefit institutions. Into our own fractured society.

And that is where the work of a psychologist must end, too. Not in the person, but through them, with them, in the decision to complain or fight harder or get together with others to have a say. In the tiny voice of value so deeply hidden, resonating with others in the community as a powerful agent of change. In the lives lived more fully, freer from fear, in enriching relationships, given to children growing into themselves.

And this, I believe, is also the inward-outward road Christ calls us to. Attentive to the least powerful, the unseen and the unsaid, costly, self-giving, beyond our control, energised by God, rhythmic and engaged with all that we see in the world. I surrender to it!

> I am making my pilgrimage
> down.
> Down to the waters of death.
>
> And although I have fought this
> nothingness,
> I find in it my very God, my very self.
>
> For here behind the busyness,
> the toil,
> the mentalism of a modern life,

is death
and birth
and the stony path down to the shore
where I and I alone
my God in me and me in my God
can tread.

My loves, my strivings, all my fierce ideals
I must lay aside.

Only the power and pain and glorious colour
of my God
to flare in me as I go down to the void,
and am caught up within
like a ribbon in the tide.

So lay me wide and enter me,
sweet waters of death, and birth.

I belong to you.
I am yours alone.
I am ready to be submerged.

Elizabeth Wild

Butterfly wings

Like a bottle of water
turned upside down
you gurgled your presence,
fluttered your wings
across my middle
somersaulting near my kidneys,
my beloved inner organ,
swimming, flying, beating
a path across my
mediterranean.
Welcome!

Ruth Harvey

Having a coffee with God and chatting about parenthood

God, I was just thinking about the intense relationship between parent and child and wondering what it can tell us about your nature.

I am in essence inter-relational.

Can you say a bit more about that please?

Everyone and everything relates to one another through me and within me. There is no relationship that is outside of me.

That statement could lead on to a whole host of other questions but now I want to concentrate on *parenthood*. Why is parenthood so hard?

Because looking at your children is like looking in a mirror and brings back painful as well as positive memories.

I often find myself doing or saying the things adults used to do or say to me as a child. Why can't I move on and be original?

There are issues from your own childhood still to be worked through, and until you do that, they will continue to influence your ability to parent.

But I had no obvious trauma or loss in my childhood. I had a very fortunate start to life with a loving family.

We all have wounds to be healed and bruises that have never completely faded. We have all felt humiliated or ignored as children. We have all experienced jealousy or rivalry of some form within our families. The list goes on …

I suppose I considered these issues to be petty and 'childish', undeserving of my attention.

Until you give whatever it is that still niggles at you from your childhood some attention, your ability to parent will be affected. Let me ask you a question. What has been one of your most profound experiences as a parent?

Losing my third child – whom we named Peter – very early in my pregnancy.

What insights did you gain from Peter?

That we bond spiritually with our children before they are even fully formed physically. That love between a mother and child is incalculable and never-ending. That to name, acknowledge and pray for an unborn child who has died brings healing and wholeness for all of the family and freedom for the child.

And ...?

And the sense of loss and pain is unimaginable. The depths of sorrow to which you plummet feel well beyond anyone else's reach. The memory of Peter and the sense that he is very much a part of our family is something ever-present in my heart.

But ...?

But since friends prayed with us and shared bread and wine, I have felt better in myself. I often picture Peter laughing on a swing. I have let him go, but he is as precious to me as are my four lovely daughters.

You faced your pain when Peter died. You stepped into a black hole and with the support of your loved ones, over many months, you found healing, wholeness and light. That same vulnerability and courage can enable you to face other issues from your past.

So basically, the more I experience healing and wholeness in my life, the more we will all benefit, children and adults.

Yes! Oh, and this listening and talking thing we're doing now helps a great deal. Not just with me but with your family.

Children *do* say the most amazing things. My third daughter, Katie, asked me, aged 5: 'Mummy, if we all love each other, then why do people need to get married?'

Children are very close to the light. They still have clarity in their thinking and an ability to see what many adults have been blinded to over the years.

How can I encourage these thoughts?

Listen to your children and accept what they tell you as being real for them, even if you don't fully understand them.

What about when they ask really profound questions?

As much as possible encourage the answer to come from within them. Ask them more probing questions. Jesus was a master at that.

Yes, that makes sense. I never feel satisfied when I merely pass on my own way of thinking. I do trust that they have the answers within themselves. I often feel that I learn a great deal more from them than they do from me.

That's good, but in reality you enhance each other's lives all the time, and you have chosen to be together in order to do so.

I do love life with all of its ups and downs, and I love our conversations. Thank you for life and love and communication.

It's my pleasure – enjoy the journey.

Shirley Billes

A depth of love and commitment

I have, or had, eight nieces and nephews: four of each. These curious and varied creatures arrived in my life within the space of almost exactly five years, from 26 October 1980 to 18 October 1985, doubling the size of my 'nuclear' family in one fell swoop. Or at least it felt like that. Every time I turned around or didn't pay attention, another baby was on the way or being born.

Their joyful arrival relieved me of any burden to produce creatures of my own! My creatures have become poems mainly, with a few other variations along the way. I never really had, or perhaps sought ardently enough, the opportunity to be a mother to my own biological children.

It is a matter of pride to me that I can still recall the date and year of birth of each niece and nephew without being entirely dependent on written reminders. I can still remember their names too! I don't expect this to last though, and not just because of my advancing age.

Sadly, the presence these children had in my life, and I had in theirs, has mostly deteriorated over the years, largely due to their enforced loyalty to parental/other adult behaviour and influence. In my family, this has often been characterised by infighting, poor communication, jumping to conclusions, lack of ability to forgive and a host of other crimes and misdemeanours.

The children are now all in their early to mid-twenties and finding their way in the world, except for a dearly cherished niece who, with the world too hard and her heart too tender, decided to leave us abruptly one October morning and took her own life. I shall miss her forever. I wonder about the month of October, a month of births and death:

Falling ... waking

Was there a moment
of epiphany, that dark morn early
when you chose to fall
into your final darkness?

If not, I hope your soul
had soared aloft
and headed home
before your outer casing
hit the earth and shattered
all our waking.

I have virtually no contact with three of my nieces and one nephew, the offspring of one deceased sibling, and another sibling bitter since that death, and many times since. Gladly, I have frequent and fond contact with one nephew, and infrequent but equally fond contact with two other nephews, who live in the USA, and whom I have visited and had visit me in Scotland a few times over the years. Relationships with my American family, though positive and loving, are only partially so but that's to do with differing religious perspectives – which is a whole other story!

Essentially, of my eight nieces and nephews, I now only have one nephew with whom I can share regular hugs, jokes, deep conversations, heated debates and differing tastes in music and hobbies. In twenty years my potential and actual lived experience of my nieces and nephews as people has been decimated. They arrived in my life in one fell swoop but have 'left' in what has seemed a crazy, confused, stuttering mixture of opportunities and challenges, raised and dashed hopes, excitements and disappointments.

I find myself wondering whether my experience is in any way akin to that of parents with their own children. While I do not claim to have known the kind of heart-rending tugs of love and war that parents of my acquaintance speak of, I do know from experience about a depth of love and commitment for my enchanting, perplexing, infuriating and challenging nieces and nephews. And for this and for them, despite the sadnesses, I am immensely grateful to God, who knows, as I now do, that their story is not yet over, even for my niece who died, in terms of their place in my life in the present and in the future.

Yvonne Morland

Letting go

It's an extraordinary business, mothering. And this is an interesting time for me to reflect on it, with our youngest having just flown off to Peru for his gap year project. So the nest is empty.

What do I feel? I certainly feel the reality of the empty nest syndrome: there is sadness; I miss the children's presence. But predominantly there is the feeling that it was time to go, time to move on, and that it was the right and best thing – both for them and me.

Which leads me to muse on the inevitable giving and letting go which is part and parcel of mothering. I have found that this draws out the deepest of emotions, a self-giving love that would not have seemed possible before the onslaught of the extraordinary and God-given gift of my children. And in the letting go there is a trust as well, a mutual trust that the relationship is there, that what matters between us will remain. But on a day-to-day basis I am no longer needed in the way I once was. Yet I am still needed, and it is still important that I am there. There in the background; there when needed. The invisible rope that once was tighter is now loose – and I'm extremely grateful for that!

I've been realising recently that there is a kind of parallel here with God, with the self-giving nature of God's love, the give and take, the leaving-us-to-it: the hoping we might just remember to keep in relationship.

Bridget Hewitt

Joy

Like a seed
In the inward arches of my body
Pressing out
Your love explodes

In the darkness of a dull day
Too cold to go out: out white frosted sting
Windows gelid with condensation
Some rooms chill and others nearly warm
Toys everywhere, a mess of food
On faces, chairs and rug
Mid screams and requests,
Pleasurable shouts aloud
And all competing demands

Like laughter
Surprised from hiding within my cavernous fears
Released
Your hope springs out

Gradual, sudden, unexpected, unrehearsed
Among the everyday of play, adventure
Exploration and the eating of fluff
This clarity at the hands
Of a feisty babe, balancing for the first time
Ecstatic, panting, rotating wide splayed hands at wrists
Full of joy and pride

Your seed of love
Your hope of laughter
In my presence held

This privilege, your glory
Finding out the tender point
That turning makes
This weary work inspired.

Elizabeth Wild

Words of Wisdom ...

... On how words, and silences, whether those of young children or of our inner child, can augment our understanding of the divine, of parenting, of self, and can lead to a place of sometimes painful, sometimes joyful understanding and insight.

Inner child

I remember as a young child discovering a clutch of small, hardbacked books on our shelves at home called *Prayers of Children* and *Children's Letters to God*. They always made me laugh, and at the age of 10 there was something voyeuristic about reading these words – if I was to write and publish a prayer or a letter to God, what would it say?

Sometime not long after that I took to writing to God myself. I'd gone through a significant house move and truly felt I would never recover: that absolutely and utterly no one in my family would ever, ever understand how I felt. Not only would they never understand how I felt about the move – they would never understand about *me* – about my likes and dislikes – about music and fashion, about love, about the world, about everything. I still have some of the letters I wrote to God then. Whether I believed God would understand me or not, I did know that I could say whatever I liked to God. I could speak from the heart. And I had a captive audience: God wouldn't be doing the dishes or going out to a meeting.

My letters to God were written at the same time as I took up a systematic and religious commitment to nightly prayer. If I hadn't prayed for each of our kittens, for all the various people in the beds around our home, and if I hadn't uttered the required number of 'for ever and ever and evers' and 'amens' then my prayers would not be answered: and something dreadful would happen: and it would all be my fault.

God was a 'great big God' out there, benevolently working and sorting things out. While in my heart I knew that God was both 'out there' and 'in here', I needed God to be *in control*. So in my head I was happy for God to be out there making judgement calls.

Scroll forward to 2003, when our first daughter got articulate, and I was back with the 'Letters to God' books of my own childhood. We went through the really funny stage of 'Mummy, why are my legs attached to my bottom', and 'When I get tired my brain starts going away' to the more winsome 'Why do some people give other people their hearts?', to (all in a oner, at the age of 3 and a half): 'What happens when you die? Are you dead when you're born? I don't want to die. Will my dolly die? Are we still alive after we die? Are we born again after we die? I don't want to die.'

My response at the time was to reassure her that she had lots of living to do: that most people died when they were old ('But I'm old, Mummy …'). And I said that inside everyone there is a little bit of God, and that even when our bodies die, that little bit of us, which is God, never, ever dies. I think then she asked if she could have more beans. Which is a child's way of saying thanks for that, now let's get on with living.

One beautiful 'letters to God' moment came at bathtime, after one child confessed that she was unhappy, and that it was the world that was making her unhappy. I offered that perhaps we could find some little things that would help make her feel happier. And immediately the younger child, by now watching and listening quietly from the bathroom doorway, reached out and said: 'She can borrow some of my little things.' This unconditional reaching out by one child to another, offering tokens of happiness in response to existential despair, surely has to be a sign of that generosity of spirit which so many of us lose to cynicism as we grow.

I try to remain alert to my children's insights about God, faith, death and love. Sometimes the misunderstandings and the shouting, the bickering and the selfishness, threaten to engulf us all – and it is then that I know that parenting is as much about putting us in touch with the dark side of our soul, as it is about connecting us with the deep and beautiful mystery of God's love.

I am waiting for the inevitable stage when our children will experience that same existential sense of aloneness felt by me at the age of 10. I hope I will have the faith, and the grace, to accompany them as they follow their own questions, their own fears and doubts, and as they encounter their God, their Jesus-companion, on the road.

This poem came during a Quaker retreat at Woodbrooke, the Quaker study centre in Birmingham. In one session we were invited to write down a 'stream of consciousness' relating an experience when one comment from a child had led us to a deeper understanding of our place in the world …

'Mummy,
are we dead before we're born?'
A three-year-old takes me to
hard talk, doubt,
intimacy,
communion,
vulnerability,
suffering.

Hard talk of politicians;
mystics who doubt;
intimacy in nursing a baby;
communion through deep sharing;
vulnerability of the excluded;
responses to suffering.

Here I am reconnected with the source,
the ground of my being.

Ruth Harvey

The journey of life and death

From the first moment we held our children we were overwhelmed at the creation of something so delicate – so beautiful and perfect to the smallest detail, and we have been thankful to God for their place in our life. They have again and again been such a source of enrichment, stimulation, motivation, creativity and challenge for our faith and belief, for our doubts and questions.

Children offer an incredibly simple and clear outlook on our world, on the way it functions and on God's place in it. We are often surprised at their questions, which seem so simple, so natural, but which are not easy to answer and require careful thought and a very clear answer (otherwise more and more questions follow!).

It is exactly through the careful and sometimes difficult process of searching for an answer to our children's questions that we discover we are actually answering our own questions as well. What is surprising about the questions is how basic they seem but how challenging they often are to answer because they can be right at the heart of faith; they are its foundation.

For example, the constant mentioning of dying: 'Why do we have to die and what happens when you die', ever since their grandfather died. The boys actually got to see him then and it was so interesting to watch Jacob (then four) climbing on grandfather, trying to tell him something and getting angry with him for not responding. However, when the nurse came and told Jacob that grandfather was asleep, Jacob quickly corrected her, saying: 'He is not asleep, he is dead.'

It was interesting to watch the process of understanding what it actually means to be dead physically. On the spiritual side it is, of course, a different matter, which can be a real struggle to explain. If Barnabas gets upset these days about dying: 'I don't want to be dead, I want to live again', Jacob calms him down by saying: 'God will take you into his world.' But Barnabas also likes to ask: 'Why do we *need* to die?' And that is a question we adults can spend our whole life pondering. The children want to know the reasons as much as we do, but it is the children who keep asking questions and who are so quick at pointing out inconsistencies.

We (adults) push so many fundamental questions to do with our faith and our being into the background for the simple reason that we know there are no easy answers. Is it not the case that we adults stop asking important questions to do with our faith because we know there are no easy answers – and also because we are afraid to face our own mortality?

Another example of children's wonderful gift of not being afraid to ask life-death-faith-relating questions, and at the same time being able to accept what comes their way, was during my husband Alan's illness, his stay in hospital and then his recuperating at home. We experienced very uncertain times then, not knowing whether Alan's treatment for leukaemia would be successful. During such a stressful and traumatic time, when one really just lives from one day to the next, having small children around is an incredible blessing and a vital distraction. Even at the age of two, Jacob kept asking questions about Alan: Why is he ill? What are the machines next to his bed for? Why is everyone so upset? And many more. I remember that he too would get anxious and worried, but never for too long. His excitement for life would very quickly take over, and it seemed as if, on the spur of the moment, all uncertainties would disappear. I needed this sudden transition constantly to be able to renew my hope and belief in the success of the treatment.

To have Jacob and then newborn Barnabas alongside me when life and death seemed so close to each other, and every day was filled with so much expectation and desire for progress, was absolutely life-saving. I believe that having them around was a source of my ability to trust God and not to despair.

Looking back now I would wish for everyone, especially at a time of difficulty, to have a childlike approach to life, in the sense of not being scared to ask questions and then being able to move on and continue to live, trust and hope.

Barnabas' favourite song at the moment is 'We are marching in the light of God', which he wants to have sung to him every night. This is a lovely way to finish a day that is always filled with such a variety of high and low points. This song is such a perfect stepping stone for our journey in faith as a family and as four individuals. It is so simple and yet so profound, describing our human, so often clumsy way of living our lives, which are firmly held in God's hands.

Lucie Miller

Walking in faith alongside children

Flossie (aged 4) asks: 'Why do you pray to God every morning?' (I'd been doing a morning discipline for Lent.)

I want this to be really good: it may stay with her, messages regarding prayer. So I say (taken from a quote I really like): 'I pray because God loves me and wants me to be close to her.'

I feel a little bit like I've dodged it – is that really why I pray? A thought went through my head yesterday – *'Am I brainwashed?'* – when I realised that I had a couple of hymn lines and words from a prayer going round and round mantra-like in my head all day long. Am I also brainwashing the children?

I do leap inside at questions like Flossie's. I see these questions as opportunities to present alternative images of God to the kids. I am so grateful for the picture of God that my mum gave me. She offered me an image of God who is homely, humorous, accepting and near. Mum's image ran counter-cultural to those that dominated: God distant, stern, angry, controlling. Even children who don't believe in God, and I've checked this out, can describe the dominant image of God: a male, authoritarian, judgemental, critical, harsh and exclusive being, living way up in the clouds, but near enough to spy on us. I nearly always use 'She' for God, or at least ask our children if they want to pray to God as 'She' or 'He'. They are going to be faced with years of hearing God as Father, as male. So I am trying in my own way to redress the balance a tiny bit, to offer a range of images/aspects of God to help them on their journey.

'Who is God?' is a question that, since about age 4, has puzzled my two children. At one point Imogen said to me, loudly on the bus, 'Is God like John Lewis?' My mind boggled! Similarly, Flossie once asked me, 'Is that man at the nursery school older than God?' – 'that man', I eventually discovered, was Robbie Burns, whom they had been talking about at Burns Day! So despite my guerrilla tactics with the female images of God, with familiar chatty prayers, they still get God as a distant, dead relic with a familiar name but no familiar face.

I also see these questions as opportunities to open up conversation about spirituality – a big word for conversations with a 4- and 6-year-old. But they really are interested (at times).

'Walking in doubt *and* faith' might be a more accurate title for this reflection. I try to be honest with the kids. My spiritual journey is not one of certainty and definitive answers. I tell them if I don't know, or if their question is really complicated for me to understand. I build my doubts into the picture for them. Does this help? I read somewhere that children need simple facts when they are young – prayers to learn, certainty. Not a tangled web of doubts and questions. But in a family where one parent prays, reads the Bible and goes to church, and the other does not, I can't pretend to be certain or to have all the answers.

And some of the questions would vex the most learned theologians: 'How exactly did Jesus come alive again?' 'Why did God not die?' 'Why/how is God alive?' 'Who is God's grandpa?' And trying to unpick exactly what the 4- or 6-year-old is wondering about is one thing. Explaining it in easy-to-understand language is another. They certainly don't want a sermon. These simple yet complex questions force me to reassess where I stand. Sometimes the answers I have seem trite, or unfathomable. I think the added pressure of being the sole source of theology in our house makes it more difficult. Then it gets really intellectual, really heady. Is what I say 'theologically correct'? Am I out of step, just making it up to suit me? Making an idol? I don't understand myself, but I know that that is why I walk in faith, not certainty, and try to live the questions.

I do like asking what they think about things. Especially Imogen, who, at six, has quite a detailed picture emerging. When she started school there was an intense phase of finding out who at school believed in God, who definitely didn't and who wasn't sure. Who prayed and who didn't. She talks about whether she'll go to church when she is an adult (at the moment she thinks not). And she is still deciding if she believes or not.

One of her best friends, let's call her Alice, is from an atheist/agnostic family. They recently moved to one of the islands in the Outer Hebrides where the Free Kirk holds a lot of influence and where expressing an opinion of not believing in God has led to bullying. I had a conversation with her when she was playing with Imogen. It started with her asking 'Do you believe in God?', and when I said 'yes' she immediately replied 'I don't' (in a fairly strong, argumentative manner I have to add!). Conversation closed.

After a few moments, I continued: 'You know, sometimes I'm not always sure what people mean when they say God, and sometimes I'm not sure myself.' I went on to say I didn't believe God was a man with a fluffy beard that lived in the sky. That actually it was nearly impossible to put my finger on what exactly I *did* mean. Which is why I usually feel on more secure ground talking about Jesus, who was a man, and because we know about lots of things he did and said. I explained that not everyone who says they believe in God means the same thing.

Alice told me about the bullying, and how much she missed her friends and old school. Alice, Imogen and I talked about what kind of man Jesus was, and agreed that he never made people feel left out. It was one of the best spiritual conversations I have ever had.

Rachael Yates

Home schooling

The end of another home schooling day in the life of the Blease family. I think bedtime is the part I will miss the most when they have grown up. It is a wonderfully cosy feeling to know that my chicks are all safely tucked in for the night. I know where they are and don't have to worry about what time they will be in. Call me a control freak, but I just love this part of mothering.

We always seem to manage to end on a good note, feeling loving towards each other, even if tempers have frayed and harsh words have been spoken during the day. There is something about the bedtime ritual, which hasn't changed much in 11 years (apart from that it has got later), that is soothing and forgiving. Brushing teeth and hair, reading stories, saying prayers – usually thinking about all we have to be thankful for or singing a song or hymn – kisses and hugs. It is a time when they love to ask thoughtful searching questions. Is this because of the pause at the end of the day which allows their minds to ponder more deeply? Maybe, and probably also because we are focused in on them face to face, saying 'goodnight' and 'I love you', rather than being busy with the chores of the day or standing with a back to them at the kitchen sink. So it is a time I treasure, and I try not to be in a hurry to get out the bedroom door to 'begin' my evening. And I live with the faith that I will grow into that scary unknown territory of children old enough to go out at night.

Experience has shown over the past 10 years of parenting that this is true. I never thought I would know how to parent an almost 11-year-old. But in all these amazing 10 years my children have been my best teachers. They say you learn more in the first three years of life than at any other time. For me the next most important phase of learning has been as a mother. Surrender and patience have been the biggest lessons I have learned and am still (sometimes painfully) learning. My children (good teachers that they are) have stuck with me every step of the way. They forgive me my mistakes but they make me keep on learning.

On the face of it, here am I, home schooling my children, when in fact I am the one doing most of the learning.

When my first son was born I had no idea what a journey of learning and spiritual growth I was about to begin. I thought I was so ready for all the challenges of parenting – I was just so excited to be a mother. I had witnessed and helped in the nurturing and upbringing of my four younger siblings and countless cousins. I had watched my mother and my aunties. I took pride in the fact that I could change a nappy at the age of six. I thought I would sail through the whole thing … And although love, dedication and enthusiasm are wonderful qualities to set out with, there were other lessons to be learned that I could have had no idea about at the time.

I was envious recently of a friend, who has just had her first baby. She has spent the last few years 'finding herself' and working out many issues in her life and from her childhood. I started thinking, *Oh, if only I had had that chance, so that I would have been more prepared and more patient*. It was that 'if only I could start over knowing what I know now' sort of feeling. It was then that I realised that, for me, it is through *being* a mother that I find myself on the path of self-discovery.

Rudolf Steiner said that the greatest gift you can give your child is that of your continued growth. I didn't arrive somewhere when I first became a mother. I embarked on a huge adventure of learning. I didn't just become a mother at the moment I gave birth. I am becoming a mother all the time, every day growing.

Victoria Blease

Tonight

Children are strange,
resilience in fragile packaging.
Wounds heal almost before your eyes,
bumps forgotten in the insistence of now.
Carried to bed with a silent prayer that Larkin is wrong.*

They tuck you up, your mum and dad.
Again and again.
Kissed foreheads a clumsy proxy
for the fierceness of this longed-for love,
sacrificial gifts.

All tenderness, all negotiation
seems so pitiful
against the wildness of this world.
The violence and betrayal
that leach through the many gaps.

Yet tonight
the lights on the tree still work.
And for the first time,
the children need no instruction.

Six busy hands,
a bustle of baubles and reverent chatter.
Parents quietly marginalised,
eyes damp at this holy sight.
Tonight, our children build hope for themselves.

* *'This Be the Verse'*, by Philip Larkin

David McNeish

Roar like a lion

I have two daughters. They have hair the colour of conkers. They have mud under their fingernails and everyone can tell they've been eating strawberries. It's July 2010. They are 7 and 9 years old. I can barely remember the nappy years now: I have to get out my photo albums. The girls love the pictures of themselves as babies. For me, it's like opening Pandora's box – those brief years of early motherhood which, for the most part, I struggled with:

Sunday, summer 2004

I'm being driven, by necessity, to look and feel in new ways, to come to appreciate the glory of life in small fists, stained faces and flannelette sheets smelling of baby. I now have to be uplifted by 'Hamish the Highland Coo' while my daughters ransack my jewellery box and empty shampoo inside. I can't say how many times I've stood beside the wall and pressed my head against it.

I'm stretched and used, loved and fought with. I come back for more again and again, like a well-strung yo-yo. I have to because my children demand it and, in spite of my old life desires, because I demand it. If I look closely enough, there's a kind of grace in my role because it's undisputed: it's clear what I have to do – be a mother.

This is what my life is now – observing, tending to and loving children, day and night. There isn't anything else. I encourage myself to view my children as works of art, unfolding novels and untrodden woodlands and myself as the one lucky enough to experience them first-hand, to look on and participate, to bear witness to their truth.

But life is like a silent film being played over and over, as though it's waiting for me to accept it for what it is; I'm meant to grow through this experience; I'm supposed to throw off my old existence, shed my old snakeskin and don this new garb. Not only that, I'm to enjoy and recommend my new life, even (needs must) find soul-food in a bowl of Rice Crispies and their masticated rejection on the floor. I sense there's a long way to go.

My old friend Christine is a child-magnet. Fern adores her, shows her more affection than she's ever demonstrated to me. I understand that she's using my friend as a power-tool to drill bloody little holes in my heart. I conceal my hurt as best I can and try to speak to Christine about how difficult I find parenting, how it often isn't enjoyable. She looks at me kindly.

'It's good fun most of the time though, isn't it?'

I nod and nod.

Giving up silence is one of the greatest sacrifices I've had to make as a parent. I yearn for those days and weeks spent on my own in bothies, building fires and sleeping with my head full of mountains. Sleeping all night. When I speak to my mother about silence, I tell her about how I miss my free time, my contemplative mind time. I tell her about walking in the woods beside the River Whiteadder and how I saw an oyster-catcher, a yellowhammer and a heron, its wings clapping the tops of the Scots Pine.

'You forget the shitty times,' she said. 'It all seems worth it in the end.'

There's a prehistoric hill fort and broch near Abbey St. Bathams and I stood inside it trying to imagine what it would have been like to live there thousands of years ago. The hillsides would have been thickly forested back then. I like to imagine a tribe of friendly folk, socialising around fires, sleeping in sheepskin beds. I don't like to think about women dying in childbirth or babies freezing to death, or the daily slog of finding firewood and food. Let's forget the shitty times.

Abbey St. Bathams was the first time in three years that I've spent more than two hours away from my children. It was my first chance to walk again, to eat my sandwich halfway up an empty hillside. I'd been looking forward to it all week, didn't anticipate crying with exhaustion, crying because I ached for my children and because I'd forgotten how much being alone in nature means to me.

Monday

By the end of the day, there is nothing left of me. I am an empty, dried-up old husk with scarcely enough energy to eat potatoes and salad before sinking into bed. All that I am, I give to my children. I am a dandelion clock, blown each day by my daughters who huff and puff until every last spore is gone.

Tuesday

It's not that I didn't think about death before my children came along, only that their arrival has suddenly shifted my perspective on age and time passing. Suddenly, the clock takes on an importance I never allotted it before. I wear a watch again, having not worn one for 10 years. Time becomes the currency with which we pay our way as parents. Time seduces and crushes me. Future time is for when everything will be easier. Past time is for when everything *was* easier. Now is a struggle to balance the needs and wants of my children with my needs and wants and those of my husband.

I've become acutely aware of time, of clocks ticking everywhere, of the alarm clock and the fact that the children always wake before it goes off.

Sunday

I feel guilty about wanting time away from my children. I crave time to be alone and yet I can't leave them behind. I feel incompetent, as though I ought to be able to stay the course, but there I am – wimp, hopeless loser – crumpled beneath it. Surely that's not me? That's not the person I thought I was, not the mother I was planning on being. She looks dour, her hair needs brushing. Someone needs to tell her, she's got Marmite on her face.

I love my children. I'd forfeit my life for them. Sometimes it feels as though that's exactly what I'm doing.

Wednesday

Am I suffering from depression? I don't want to be depressed. Worrying about being depressed makes me more depressed. I'm stuck in a tiny vault. If people ask me how I'm feeling, tears prick my eyes.

Rebecca phoned and we chatted superficially about our families, our lives. I was caught between wanting to regain the close link I once had with her by being honest, and not wanting to burden her with my stuff. In spite of myself, I couldn't hold back the tears. She sounded embarrassed or just didn't know what to say.

Friday

I'm reading Adrienne Rich's *Of Woman Born*:

> *'Even today, rereading old journals, remembering, I feel grief and anger; but their objects are no longer myself and my children. I feel grief at the waste of myself in those years, anger at the mutilation and manipulation of the relationship between mother and child, which is the great original source and experience of love.'* [1]

I want to write and ask her how she could have done it differently, how not to have wasted herself. In the meantime, I'm waiting to feel more fulfilled, but it's an endless waiting, a nonsense almost. What more fulfilled?

> *'If you can't find the truth where you are, where else do you expect to find it?' Dogen (founder of Japanese Zen)*

The truth is, I'm not fulfilled as a mother. Some days, most days, I wish I could do something else; I wish I could write. But I don't need to be fulfilled to live a life. Life isn't about fulfilment or the attainment of happiness. It's so difficult to accept misery, to accept that there's a suppressed part of me because I don't have head-space from my children or time to be creative. That's OK, isn't it? It's not a waste, it just is. It just is.

Mother

No hushed cradle beneath apple trees,
no puddle-ducks quacking at the back door,
only snail-paced fontanelles shifting

into a new continent of child:
all arms and hands and oceanic voice.

You say *ooh* and *aah* and mock
in a way only a mother dare:
tut tut and how long is my daughter's hair?
But you never told me I'd be stranded with her,
sand in my eyes, you never, island heart.

Sunday

I have moments of adoration and contentment when I see them sitting in
the garden together, feeding each other raspberries.

Wednesday

I'm reading Rozsika Parker's *Torn in Two*, which is excellent. Of maternal
ambivalence, she writes:

> *'Such painful truths can only be expressed through humour; it is only via
> irony and a light touch that ambivalence is rendered bearable.'* [2]

I don't agree. Ambivalence makes it bearable. I find it comforting that
there's this swinging and switching of emotions; almost as though, if I
didn't have the ability to move between the two, I'd drown in the one,
stagnate. Ambivalence keeps the relationship vital and enables human
beings to grow. I don't find it tragic or unbearable. I find it real and
wonderfully, imperatively human.

Sunday

My life has gone. There is nothing left now that resembles my life before
children. I am changed utterly – my surroundings, my priorities, my
(non) choices, all changed. There is this new identity trying to force
itself on to the old one, to snuff out the non-mother. Struggle, struggle to
keep hold of some of the old, to hold tight to who I am, what I need
beyond the existence and needs of my children.

I never once thought motherhood would bring this. The constant nappies, tears, tantrums, battles of will, whingeing, sleep deprivation, none of it has surprised and challenged me, has made me suffer so much as has the transition to a new identity.

'Mothering can make a woman feel profoundly childish … Interesting that a psychoanalytical approach to the mother-child relationship sees a child-child scenario where the mother actually becomes herself a child again – in a profoundly negative sense, inasmuch as she feels angry and frustrated at having her own needs disallowed. She tantrums. She feels hard done by and sulky.' [3]

Tuesday

My dear friend Esther gives herself treats when she's feeling bogged down with the kids and I wondered why I hadn't thought of that: 5 minutes silence; a walk on the beach alone; a cappuccino with chocolate on top. Until I discovered that her treats weren't treats at all, but acts of surrender: she gives up whatever plans she had for the day, agrees to lose the battle with her toddler, in order to sit down by the radiator and have a cup of tea! Right. Great.

'If nothing else works,' she said, 'then I tell my girls I'll be leaving the room for a minute, and I roar like a lion. It works every time: I get to release the anger and frustration and the girls are moved away from the dilemma by my brief departure. Sometimes they even laugh: "Mummy, Mummy, why are you roaring?"'

I tried roaring in our house but it wasn't as successful. My girls cried and shook, as though a real lion had leapt from her cage, teeth bared. Perhaps I should have roared in the garden instead.

Thursday July 29th, 2010

The transition to motherhood has taught me far more about myself, about human nature and about love, than any other single experience in my life. I feel immense gratitude for this. It's only now that I realise my children have awakened in me the capacity to truly accept and deeply love.

Small last girl

Small last girl at the gorilla gates to school,
your hand in mine still,
your backpack big as a straw-bale.

It's the wind that tips my heart
into the ditch, blows it –
pleading red muscle –
into the sycamore
where it mewls and waits
for the fire brigade to put it out.

I drive for a bit into town,
spot my middle years in shop windows,
buy an ice cream that tastes of soap.

When you come home
you stick peonies in a vase,
spill me a cup of tea
and tell me about
the fire in the tree
how the firemen *extigwisht* it
with real yellow helmets on
that reminded you of daffodils.

Yesterday we walked to the loch and the girls swam out to the raft with their friends. They found two swan feathers in amongst the reeds and lily pads. Afterwards we sat on the shore and ate chocolate muffins and apricots. Someone was out on the water learning to windsurf. 'Is that what you do, Mum, just pull on the rope, stand on the board and then fall in? It looks fun.' 'Well, yes, but once you've mastered it, you actually get to sail all the way across the loch.'

Em Strang

Notes:

1. *Of Woman Born: Motherhood as Experience and Institution,* by Adrienne Rich,
W.W. Norton & Co., 1996
2. *Torn in Two: Maternal Ambivalence,* by Rozsika Parker, Virago Press, 2005
3. *Torn in Two: Maternal Ambivalence,* by Rozsika Parker, Virago Press, 2005

My journey

My faith journey might have been less tortuous, albeit less interesting, if I had been born with the wit to understand and document its stages in a clear and consecutive manner. But I wasn't, and when I try to reflect on the stages of this journey all I see is muddle. I can't think in terms of my faith – its ebb and flow, its waxing and waning – without getting it mixed up in my head with the entire muddle of my life, the jumble of longings, fears, disappointments and hopes around my mothering, my vocation as a working artist, my friendships, my sexual relationships. Reaching into the roots of my spiritual nature is inseparable from my persistent reaching into the roots of all that wounds me, hurts me, gives me joy, and impels me to express myself. I am unable to separate out the strands.

There have been periods in my life when I have been a devout Christian, at times verging on fundamentalism. There have also been times when my spiritual journey has been characterised by aridity. And mostly I have found myself somewhere in between. The path is however not straight. Early in 2005, I was very influenced by a book called *The Gospel According to Woman* by Karen Armstrong, in which she documents the history of the Christian church's hatred of and fear of sexuality through the ages, and how this hostility towards our sexual nature reached its most nightmarish expression in witch burnings. She outlines the way in which such fear of sexuality has shaped us all, and our relationships, whatever our sexual proclivity. My reading of this book coincided with a period of bereavement, when I was grief-stricken by my partner's decision to end our relationship after seventeen years together. The bitterness of this experience, combined with the reading of this book which threw into relief the nature of much that had torn us apart, brought me to a place of great aridity in my faith journey. As my grief eases, I find that my relationship with my Christian inheritance continues to change, and I find myself wondering about the relationship between grief and faith, and need and faith. But I am no theologian. What I do understand however is that our need for a sense of meaning shapes all of our actions, however much we might wish to dress them up, and knowing that this is basic to my humanity frees me, paradoxically in spite of the somewhat sordid nature of such a realisation, into an acute knowledge of my absolute need for grace. Who provides this grace is the gnawing question. Is it God, or is it the angels? Or is it my relationship with Jesus Christ which redeems me? I can't say. But I know it's happening. I am in no doubt that I am not alone.

As a child I was very serious, very bookish, very sad, very dutiful. My mother was a devoted and upright woman, as well as being fun-loving. She was deeply religious, and we were packed off to Sunday school every Sunday. I say 'packed off' because I hated going, and am always amused to read Liz Lochhead's poem 'The Offering':

> Never in a month of them
> would you go back.
> Sunday,
> the late smell of bacon
> then the hard small feeling
> of the offering in the mitten.
> Remember how the hat-elastic cut.
> Oh the boredom,
> and how a lick of spittle got purple dye or pink
> from the hymn-book you worried …[1]

Wonderful, and absolutely how it felt for me in every detail. Most people who read this are probably too young to remember those rigid feather alice-bands which we wore, and which gave me a headache, Sunday after Sunday. Sunday was also the day on which – being so dutiful – I cleaned out my goldfish tank – and I loathed this job with a passion! We were fortunate to be brought up in the lovely and historic parish of Cockpen, and although I loathed the Sunday school, I loved the old church, and I loved the activities which went with one's membership – the Christmas parties, the concerts in which we all had a part, our proud parents in the darkened audience – if we were lucky to have parents, or to have parents who cared enough to come and see our performance. I was lucky – my mother did care – but not so lucky to have lost my father when I was five years old.

In my teenage years I became somewhat fanatical in my religious lean-ings, and agonised over many of the scriptures, for example the parable of the sheep and the goats. I could not reconcile myself to a God who would punish some and save others. How could this be reconciled to the inequality into which children are born, the circumstances over which we have no control, and which can release a child into a life of creativity or, conversely, bury him/her in a life of destruction, towards others or self or both.

In July 1976 I went to Iona as part of a student group. Two formative moments from this first visit to Iona were hearing John Harvey preach in the Abbey about little children, that their 'innocence' was not defined by their inherent goodness but by the fact that they were devoid of status-consciousness. And the second vivid memory was hearing Graeme Brown speak about his experience of living and teaching in South Africa during the time of apartheid. The fresh and fearless nature of their words helped begin for me a process of liberation from my spiritual 'strait-jacket'. I became a member of the Iona Community some years after this first visit.

In those early years of my membership I was a young mother of two, and the boys and I spent time on the island every year of their young lives. My younger son Mike likes to boast about the number of times he has been to Iona, latterly as a volunteer. He has gone from strength to strength, most recently deciding to pursue a course in dramatic art, and he would attribute his growth in confidence to his 'Iona experience'. He is a great devotee! Tim, my elder son, lives a life of breathtaking commitment to the values that the Iona Community embraces, and much of his work nowadays takes place on the African continent, bringing him back full circle to those members, especially those who had known and loved Africa, who supported him so generously when he spent his gap year in South Africa in 1998. Tim is a practising church-goer, whereas Mike and I are not. But we are all, in our several ways, influenced deeply by our Christian heritage, and Iona has provided a loving and accepting, as well as demanding, context in which the boys have been able to express their search for their spiritual roots without embarrassment or apology, in this secularised age when young people are often mocked for their religious beliefs.

In recent years, in response to much heart-searching and prayer, I have been increasingly able to affirm the God-given nature of my vocation as a visual artist, to experience the conviction that the energy which moves between myself and the people and images I draw and paint and the energy which moves and breathes throughout my struggle for spiritual understanding are one and the same energy; and for this and my understanding of this role in terms of my commitment to peace and justice, I am grateful. My membership of the Iona Community has played a significant role in my journey along this road to gratitude and healing.

Joyce Gunn Cairns

Note:

1. 'The offering', by Liz Lochhead, from *Dreaming Frankenstein and Collected Poems*, Liz Lochhead, Polygon Books, 1984

I know a cat whose name is ...

There's a stigma to mental illness – still. People empathise but then back off. Like they suddenly smell something on you, like they're afraid of contagion.

People wonder why you don't just snap out of it. It's maddening – you can't snap out of it! You can't snap out of hell. On the outside you look in and don't believe, or want to believe, it could happen to you. Well, it can.

In 1996 I went through an 'episode' of clinical depression. I lost all confidence in myself, couldn't work for much of the time; I broke up with my partner – actually, she broke up with me; who can blame her? I'd become irritable, manipulative, needy as a child. At one point the depression got so bad that I started to self-harm, to cut the insides of my arms with kitchen knives. I'd tell people that the cat did it. I was just playing with the cat. I was playing with death.

How did I fall down so far? How did I go from someone who had worked as a nurse's aide and a counsellor, from someone who'd travelled through Yugoslavia solo, to someone who couldn't even take a city bus alone? … One thing was certain: I was sure that, down below, it was my fault. It wasn't of course, but I couldn't help feeling that I was a very weak person. Weak, defective, lazy, a loser. A failure: the shame of depression on top of the depression.

I did a lot of things to survive during that time: I talked to good friends, I fell back on family, I went through counselling, I took anti-depressants. One day, I woke up and started writing children's poems. I had always written, but I'd never once thought of writing children's poems. I was desperate. I was clawing for the light.

The depression lasted for about a year and a half, maybe longer. I've been well since that time. These days I feel blessed: I have work I feel passionate about, a wonderful partner; sometimes I even do gigs as a stand-up comedian. If you had told me, back in the days when it was hard to get out of bed in the morning, that one day I'd be doing stand-up comedy, I never would have believed you.

Sometimes when I'm doing stand-up, I use the following poem in my act – one of the 'children's poems' I wrote when I was clinically depressed. I recite the poem and skip rope. Punters seem to enjoy it. That a poem I wrote when I was clinically depressed now makes people laugh is a miracle to me.

On the surface, this little poem may seem to have nothing at all to do with being a survivor of depression; for me, though, it is an embodiment of 'the light that shines in the darkness' …

Going through depression has rooted my faith, has brought me closer to Jesus Christ – I have no problem in the world now in believing in resurrection.

I used to feel very guarded and ashamed talking about mental illness. Now I need to hold myself back. I want to shake people awake and tell them how close to the edge we can all come, how normal it is – how human.

Skipping song

This poem is a performance piece. When I recite it in a club, I do things like throw peanuts, drink milk, hand cans of tuna fish and salmon to the audience …

I know a cat whose name is Mimi
she doesn't like tuna fish
I know a cat whose name is Mimi
what's her favourite dish?

(skip:)

Pears Potatoes
Pizza pie
Falafels Capers
Ham on rye

Olives Pickles
Fried bananas
Rumballs Gumballs
Dried sultanas.

I know a cat whose name is Mingy
who likes his mozzarella stringy

I know a cat whose name is Leroy
who left the duck and ate
the decoy

I know a cat named Siamese Sam
who's lost his yen for corned beef and Spam
I know a cat named Siamese Sam
what sticks to his chops?

(skip:)

Blue cheese
Toasted fleas
Chocolate-covered honeybees

Garter snakes
Frosted flakes
Pistachio-almond honeycakes.

I know a cat named Need-a-tail
who's trying to eat a lot of kale

I know a cat whose name is Oopik
who forgets how to hunt walrus and seal
I know a cool cat named Oopik Topik
what's his favourite meal?

Cheese nachos All dressed tacos
Enchiladas Fried iguanas
Beef burritos Fried Tostitos
Corn tortillas Margaritas
Hot peppers! (skip like mad)

I know a cat whose name is Kate
who plays with the sunlight on her plate

I know a cat whose name's Mad Manx
who struts from his bowl and never says thanx

I know a cat titled Rex the Third
who says that eating canned food's absurd
I know a cat titled Rex the Third
what does he rather fancy?

(skip:)

Pheasant
Quail
Chinchilla under glass

Bouillabaisse
Mayonnaise
Refined sugar.

I know a Tom who's a tough Maine Coon
who picks at the garbage and cries at the moon

I know a cat named Davy Crocket
who keeps liquorice jerky in his pocket

I know a cat who's an opera singer
and always wears black coat and tail
I know a cat, half-alto, part-tenor,
what does he like for dinner?

(skip:)

Rigatoni
Rice-a-roni

Fried baloney
Cold spumoni
Manicotti
Pavarotti

Late Puccini
Hot linguine

Cannelloni
Macaroni

Vermicelli
Cold spaghetti

Hot peppers!! *(skip like mad)*

I know a cat who likes a good pot luck
I know a cat who likes a good pot lick

I know a cat who smelt the smelts
(in the salty, fishy, kitcheny air)

I know a cat who's fond of airline peanuts

I know a cat whose name is Stevie
who crunches on Spice Mice watching late-night TV

I know a cat called Hate-to-Cook
who'd rather shed on her deep, soft bed
I know a cat named Hate-to-Cook
what does she like instead?

(skip:)

Takeout
Drive-through
Ready to eat

Dine in
Phone-up
Delivery free

I know a cat who likes to lie
and dream of eating pie in the sky

I know a cat called Judy Star
who lives for caviar by soft guitar
I know a feline called Judy Star

I know a cat who's kinda finicky
I know a cat who's kinda picnicy
I know a cat who sucks out the marrow
I know a cat who picks like a sparrow

I know a jaded Abyssinian
who doesn't want to eat the same thing again

I know a cat who hisses at hot dogs
I know a cat who relishes relishes

I know the cat who owns Captain Cat Burgers
(but his name is Ed)

I know a cat who chatters for chocolate
I know a cat who's a milkaholic

I know a cat named Alabamy Sammy
whose vit'ls consist of grits and groats
I know a cat named Hamish McCaindish
who always eats stiff Quaker Oats

I know a cat who skips double Dutch
and never even stops for lunch
I know a cat who skips much double Dutch

(skip:)

and never even stops for lunch
and never even stops for lunch ...

Neil Paynter

The darkness creeps up

The darkness creeps up on me
and catches me unawares.
Often just after love and laughter and hope
enfold me.
The light flickers,
the ache intensifies,
the old records
play disturbing melodies.
The dancing shadows threaten to engulf me.
An inner voice cries out:
    'You're the one to blame.
    Your reactions are at fault.
    You haven't enough patience.
    Your faith is a sham.
    You! You! You!'
I get up in the dark,
find my way to the kitchen
and eat a mince pie at 5am.
Strangely comforted
I choose to creep back into the dark
and hope that laughter and love and hope
might be reborn
as a new day dawns.

But tears flow freely now
and sobs shake my very being
as I confess that
I dearly love the child
but hate the Down's Syndrome
which disables her
and makes me feel
disabled, impotent, sad and helpless.

Katy Owen

Sunday morning house still asleep

Tree says be rooted
little flower says bloom
bird says fly before it's cold

Wind says float free
sun says Love
rain says it's OK to cry.

Neil Paynter

Made in God's Image ...

... On how the presence of children in our lives helps us to recognise afresh God as parent, and God as the incarnate, risen son, in our children, in ourselves, in the 'other'.

Disputed territory

Who is God? How do we describe the divine and still hold the mystery that gives us birth? I have battled in my adult years with the very real 'face' of God I drew as a child. In my attempts at that time to understand the cosmos I went through a period of understanding the world through diagrams. I had a very clear image of how, for example, a typical week looked, with Mondays (yellow) at the bottom left of a rectangle, Wednesday (orange) at the thin end, and God (with dark curly, male hair) in the centre. I think this image went hand in hand with the very real picture of Jesus in my primary school: Jesus wearing blue, with blond hair and blue eyes, surrounded by squirrels and birds from an English forest.

Later, prayers and reflective meditations helped me discover images of God as mother, as soul-friend, as companion, as love, as light. But somehow these childhood pictures of the creator God, and the son Jesus, have been the longest-lasting and most pervasive.

Being in the almost constant company of young children now, I wonder about the faces of God I as an adult am exposing them to. I give thanks for the many Quaker and other influences surrounding our girls that open up, rather than close down, images of the divine. At the same time, I reflect on how being around children augments my own images of God and helps free me from the limited images of my early childhood:

Dancing with angels

Child –
you are my burning bush.
Resting my eyes on you I see God
and the angels
swirling
whirling in around you.

Girl –
you are my still small voice.
In your gentler pace
in your 'Go slower, Mummy'

I hear the sound of God (and the angels)
listening
in the spaces between us.

Babe –
your footsteps are my holy ground.
Angels sing from your eyes, your lips,
through your giggle,
in your gently sleeping breath.

In my rushing,
I lose eye contact,
I dance a different dance.

You are the sacred ground of my being.
Let us touch, skin to skin –
me, stripped naked of my shield of busyness.
And let us dance an angel dance together,
and meet God, face to face.[1]

One of the faces of God which strongly speaks to me as a parent is God as companion, God as the one who accompanies us daily through life: God as the mother hen who broods over her chicks, who accompanies the little ones as they grow to independence; God as companion to Jesus, giving life and freedom. Jesus as companion, as the one with and through whom we break bread. Jesus who beckoned community around him, who sought out the marginalised, the women and the children; the risen Christ who accompanies the disciples on the road, in silence and in times of confusion.

Hearing stories from those who have taken part in the Ecumenical Accompaniment Programme in Palestine and Israel (EAPPI), where accompaniment means standing beside Palestinians being refused entry to their olive groves, or sitting on the bus alongside the fearful children who may be stopped and searched at any moment, I realise that parenting is a form of accompaniment. We stand alongside our children, being with them in the midst of heartache and celebration, witnessing to their lives, but not living their lives for them. And as a parent of young children, sometimes our very bodies can feel like disputed territory:

Disputed territory

Two peoples, two histories:
One land, one story, bearing
the battle scars of the struggle.
Enemies, yet friends sitting
side by side – both staking
their equal and inalienable claim
to the soil.

Two little girls, two histories:
One lap, one mother's body –
space each wants to occupy
wholly, to which each has
her equal and inalienable right.

No road map here will resolve
the unresolvable.
Only a heartfelt resolution
to love,
and to learn again,
as a child,
to share.

Ruth Harvey

Note:

1. First published in *Acorns and Archangels: Resources for Ordinary Time – The Feast of the Transfiguration to All Hallows'*, Ruth Burgess (ed), Wild Goose Publications

Heaven in my arms: a meditation on the Magnificat

I was 31 years old, we'd been married 2 years and he was a planned baby.

When Tom, our firstborn, decided to make an appearance, it was a fine, autumnal night. I counted minutes between pains, took a long bath, rang the hospital and was advised about the right time to go in. Then, they cared for me. And I had painkillers on hand, gas and air, a veritable rush of medics when things got tricky. Then a cup of tea, a clean bed, with the baby in a see-through crib close by, and the luxury of a bed bath, peace and sleep. I wasn't allowed visitors until visiting time and, to be quite honest – I wasn't looking my best! And I treasure the memory of that time in my heart.

Many times since, I have wanted to write it all down, to tell Tom in a letter how we shared that special time, and to share some of my thoughts over the years. About when we have fallen out, when we have had a specially good time, when things have been said, or unsaid. I would have liked to crystallise in a letter how I am proud of him, how he makes me feel sad or happy or hurt sometimes – how much I love him.

But I don't, I just treasure those moments and ponder them in my heart. Like Mary, who treasured the words of the shepherds and pondered on them in her heart. Mary holds in her memory the important events and significant moments in the drama of the Incarnation. She was there at the very beginning of the new era of God's saving events, the pivotal point at which God's new work through Jesus began.

But perhaps all those things she had stored in her heart only made sense to her much later, perhaps only at Pentecost at the birth of the new Church. But I often wonder how she would have told her story if she had written it down. Would she begin …?

Dear Jesus,

I wondered at that angel's message:

'He will be great. He will be called the Son of the Most High. Of his kingdom

there will be no end.' So it seemed it was to be *my* task to welcome you – the Creator of earth and sea and sky as a new created being, a baby. And for this, I bore the disapproval of my family and the neighbours, not to mention the distress of Joseph.

I carried and cradled you inside me from Nazareth to Judea and back again, to the well, to the market, about the daily round of chores, until we set out for the census in Bethlehem. I refused to be ashamed but was filled with amazement and hope.

Such hope.

I somehow knew my destiny was going to be shaped by my baby, but I couldn't be sure how. And I knew that the destiny of others would be transformed too; so I sang songs for you in my heart about freedom, about the world turned upside down, about the rich sent away empty and the poor and hungry filled with good things. But I also realised you wouldn't be wholly mine, and I remembered my foremother Hannah and the song she sang when her beloved Samuel was born.

She knew he was to be special, too. A servant of God.

Of course, it *would* happen that we had to travel for the census just at the wrong time. You were due, and it was as though, even then, you had already decided to ally yourself with the homeless, the poor, the lonely and the outcast … for that is just what we were.

We were tired from travelling, from the roadblocks, the searches by the soldiers. If only they had realised who I was carrying! We had nowhere to stay, and so, son, you were born in a shed, amongst strangers and animals. I was very young and frightened and it hurt, but when I held you, I knew that I was holding heaven in my arms. It was as though even the stars were singing.

And what happened after you arrived amazed me! I was feeling tired, lonely, rather dirty, very hungry, and overwhelmed, not only by just having given birth to my firstborn son in an inconvenient place at a very young age – but by all these rough, strange visitors talking excitedly about angels singing and praising God the messiah being born. There were times when I didn't really believe it was all happening: Who was I, after all? Why single me out for a special blessing? I often wondered if I'd misread the signs, or imagined it all, and there was a part of me that hoped I had. But I *wanted* to believe it more than you'll ever know … the promise that my child would 'be great, and will be called the Son of the Most High'.

We had been waiting for such a leader, but I hadn't given a moment's thought to the possibility that this messiah would be born as a baby and from someone as unimportant as I was. But the signs said someone great had been born that night, in that shed. Even the king was nervous. And the signs continued. Simeon at the temple held you in his arms and cried for joy. He said he was holding the Lord's salvation: a light for the Gentiles and for the glory of His people Israel. He also told me a sword would pierce *my* soul, too. I suppose we open ourselves up to that possibility the moment we begin to love.

And that has always brought difficulties. Love.

It's a difficult burden to bear, to love the world better, and my soul was pierced many times as I watched whilst you tried to do it. There we were, the great nation, God's chosen people, thinking this great leader would come to show the strength of his arm and scatter the proud and bring down the powerful … But we didn't really understand, did we? Your way of doing things was not with the strength of war or divine wrath and judgement, but simply with love.

Your love for others has been the way of transforming lives. You have loved to death. But I, too, bore some part of that holy burden, for I gave you my heart, my honour, my flesh and blood, and all the strength of my love.

At first I contained you, but you soon outgrew me, beyond my reach. And I had to trust, watch over you with my love and prayers, and follow you in faith, even to Calvary.

Again and again I have felt the blade of the sword piercing my heart.

Again and again I have seen your love working to transform, to turn the expectations of the world upside down, to upset warped values, to over-turn the power of the oppressors.

You taught us that war and violence solve nothing; that the only way to change things is through the power of love. You taught us that the night you were born and have gone on doing so. I have always been so proud of you, so blessed.

And now you are gone, but your loving presence is always with us. And I will always treasure the memories of that starry night when love was born.

Lis Mullen, Christmas 2002

Passionate mothering

The emotions that I experience when I write concerning motherhood are so strong that I find it difficult to express them in words. How can you express your passion for your child? Compare picking her up from nursery to meeting up with a long lost lover? But for me, that's how it was. And the anger! The anger over decisions made even with a much-loved husband. Again, very difficult to express.

And why all these passionate emotions? Because, on reflection, I am passionate about many things in my life: cooking, hillwalking, friends, godchildren, my animals, azaleas …

How then could I not be passionate about those I love most?

When people told me that the main reason I stayed at home to look after my children was because my husband had a good salary, inferring that it was something of a luxury, I thought they must be from another planet.

I would have lived on fifty pounds a week rather than be parted from my daughters – whose big, blue eyes – whose every move – brought a sense of awe and wonder.

'Poor children,' you must be thinking – what a suffocating, over-involved mother. I probably was. But I poured much of that passion into cooking, which was hugely appreciated by the children too, so that became a shared passion.

The children are now no longer children and – surprise surprise – they have their own passions: one for music and one for sport.

When all is said and done, all we can do is our best. (But then that is another passion/compulsion …)

How I envy those who can travel through life on a much lighter plane than I can. Those who can keep things in proportion, pop out the children without too many problems, and who don't bother too much about table manners.

I have watched their children grow alongside mine and have realised that all our children reflect the love they have received, and as young adults are giving it back in abundance. The academic standards, the table manners, it's all window dressing, and yet how important it all seemed at the time.

The bottom line is the ability to give and receive love, and however you are as a mother – passionate, light-hearted or whatever – you are your own child's mother. They are part of you and have 50% of your genes. They are programmed to understand you.

Middle age brings with it a certain acceptance of who we are as individuals and inevitably this will reflect on how we see ourselves as mothers. Me – passionate and probably over-involved. And yet I can honestly say that my daughters are two of my very best friends, and if they can accept me as I am then that is the icing on the cake.

Pass me the wooden spoon!

Flo MacIntyre

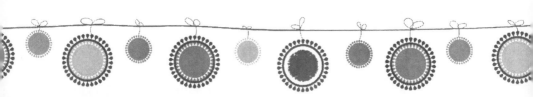

A hymn for Father's Day

(Tune: Bunessan)

Child in the manger,
friend of the stranger,
mothered by Mary,
conceived by God.
Part of a family,
loving and holy,
how we adore you,
Jesus, our Lord.

Suckled by Mary,
nurtured by Joseph,
learning his trade with
hammer and wood.
Taught by his father
to make yokes easy,
as a good joiner
certainly should.

Today we thank you
for our own fathers,
who with our mothers
teach us your ways;
loving and guiding,
always providing,
hoping and praying,
singing your praise.

Thus may we honour
father and mother,
those you have given
for us to love.
May they be treasured,
gratefully cared for,
while our life's measured
by God above.

Murdoch MacKenzie

Is this not Joseph's son?[1]

Joseph,
in the shadows,
silent,
scarcely mentioned Joseph,
omitted from the first family pictures, Joseph,
where are you,
who are you,
why have we lost you,
Joseph?

Why have we idealised Mary into a virginal icon,
Holy Mother of God Mary,
Virgin Mary,[2]
pure, innocent Mary?
Where is the menstruating woman,
the breadmaking woman
within the quest for doctrinal orthodoxy?

And we have lost you, Joseph,
your humanity,
your being man,
your fathering,
the fathering of your child,
the fathering of our child,
and all
for fear of what?

It was old Doris Moon in Notting Hill,
who never knew her mother, nor her father,
who lived her early growing years in institutions,
and all her working life 'in service',
it was Doris who gave that farewell gift,
a print of a painting sent for in Paris.[3]

Dear old Doris Moon,
with what mysterious intuition could she have known?
The painting was of you, Joseph.
No halos, no angels.

Your form,
glimpsed in the darkness,
your face, his face
lit through flickering light,
a candle in his hand.

And within the daily sounds of the workshop
your heart is heard,
your watchfulness,
your attentiveness,
listens your child into being.

Were you as the painting shows,
thick in body frame,
arms like tree trunks,
hands strong yet gentle,
face bearded, weather-beaten,
radiant, grief-stained,
a well-lived-in face,
forged through interiority
lived alongside the river of the inner cave.
Treasures also found,
heart also pierced.

Joseph,
handler of wood, worker with nails,
trusted tradesman, master craftsman of Nazareth?
Mary's man,
house-builder, home-maker
love-maker, rough, tender,
intimate man?

And what of your fathering
throughout those hidden years:
the hand-holding,
the addressing of soul,
the standing in his tracks?

What of your fathering through the awakening:
his rising and falling and rising yet again,

his playfulness,
his stretching out,
his reaching deep,
the knowing and the unknowing
the painful acquisition of life wisdom
the fearful learning of where faithfulness could lead?

Did you teach him to grow into the 'Abba' prayer,
the childhood evening prayer,
'Father into your hands I commend my spirit'?[4]
Joseph, whom do you see
when you look into the face of your child?
What of the son who has grown beyond you?

Joseph,
does not the eternal Spirit still
hover over the primal chaos,
bring light through the world's darkness,
still breathe life within the dust of the earth,
ignite the fires of passion,
fertilise through the desire
that lies beyond the heat of human desire,
still transform through our flawed mortality?

Joseph,
well-earthed Joseph,
can you help us with our rough animality?
Can you father us into being,
a birthing within our complex fragility
born again into our own resilient humanity?

Dear old Doris Moon,
who never knew her mother,
nor her father,
with what mysterious intuition could she have known?

Dear Doris,
thank you for the gift of Joseph,
Father Joseph.

Donald Eadie[5]

Notes:

1. Luke 4:22
2. I am told that for the Jew the emphasis in the word 'virgin' is not only the girl, the maiden, and that the word does not necessarily denote sexual abstinence ... but rather 'one who is genuine, with integrity, transparent, providing a glimpse of God, dedicated'.
3. Georges de La Tour's *Christ with St Joseph in the Carpenter's Shop* (painted in the late 1630s, now in the Musée du Louvre, Paris)
4. Luke 23:46
5. My birth father was named Joseph, and in recent years I have learned that he was a master builder. Our grandson is also named Joseph and has perhaps inherited some of his great grandfather's craft.

What are you thinking, Grandad?

I am who I am …

> … because I am the fruit of an ancestral tree whose roots reach back through history – whose branches stretch out to the known and unknown world;

> … because the ancestral chain of genes continues to struggle for everlasting life, in me;

> … because of a host of friends and loved ones, teachers and pathfinders, inspirers and encouragers who have shared the fruits of their inherited, developed and embodied spiritual genes;

> … because of the Divine in whose image I am fleshed out – the one in whom all I am and all I shall be lives, moves and has its being.

In me, many people meet and strive to be one – all within the Divine ambience.

> The feet of many generations shuffle with their gifts to my door.
> Where I live is now where they live –
> they in me and the potential I in them!
> The past and the future meet in me and celebrate the now.
> The sands flow in and run out –
> to those whose lives I touch, to family and friends,
> to *their* families and friends, and in the touching flow
> there is a Divinity that shapes our ends and our beginnings …

I am awestruck when I map the way by which I have come to be who I think I am. I give thanks for individual people to whom I am eternally joined.

May I be grateful for the past while letting it go. So may I be fully present where I am and to those I am with, whether they share my genes or not.

What gifts have I received to enjoy!

The loving touch of partner,
the loving concern of children now grown,
the innumerable loving words and smiles and embraces
along the road.

With what inner conflicts have I been left! In what struggles have I been invited to take my place!

And my response?

Out of the struggle comes the mixture – the good, the bad and the ugly, the perverse and the beautiful.

May the one whom I call God, whose image is in me, forgive all that needs to be forgiven between us, between my ancestors and me, between my family and me, and between myself and me. May the hurts of my history be healed and may I learn to live with the missed opportunities of my past.

Who do I think I am? I am a mix of past, present and future – wayfarer, friend, brother, husband, father, grandfather …

Today I am glad about those who have been on the journey with me so far but I am especially thinking about those who follow … my children … my grandchildren … in whom the mingling of journeys, gifts and struggles goes on …

What gifts do I bequeath them?
What potential do I pass on to them?
What little blessings do I give in and through
my relationship with them?

I see them and I see myself in them … the physical attributes … the manner in which they do things … their humour …

I see their difference – and I rejoice in them … these new creations. They are not me but they carry my image and the image of their ancestors.

Is this what it is to be God: all people carrying God's image … and God carrying the images of all of them?

May I notice what inspires and enthuses other people, and may I see a reflection of God in them – often surprising and disguised. Grant me joy in the face of difference, rather than defensiveness which hints at my possession of 'truth'. Let me see, through others, the God beyond our god and be seduced into Truth.

My grandchildren:

teach me humility …
ask for help, then tell me they will manage fine by themselves …
show me priorities (some food dropped on the carpet
is not the end of the world) …
show me unconditional love …
are a joy and are exhausting …
I am proud of their talents and
how well they are doing with their lives …

They are my grandchildren but they are not mine!

What I offered my children without choice, theirs and mine, I now offer through them to my grandchildren with a freer choice, these questing and questioning bundles of life energy, these mixes of genes and jeans.

What do I give them? What *have* I given them? What are the emotional and spiritual equivalents of what I have already given them physically and psychologically?

I trust that, through me, and in spite of me, I pass on life by the loving touch and the intimate entering into the life of another, and from that one flesh, mind and spirit springs new life!

New life, yet life in the image of all who have gone before and all that is – two rivers and countless tributaries flowing and gifting and struggling – and living!

Grandfather God,
help me to learn from my children,
their children
and all children.

Help me to be childlike enough to be:
aware of what goes on around me, whether I understand it or not –
for that is where I will see glimpses of you;

open to other people, whether I like them or not –
for that is where I will see your image and likeness;

and unashamed to be who I am,
grateful for those in the past,
loving towards those who are present.

For I know that I am surrounded by accepting love
and that you are a very
grand father.

Ken Lawson

Maintaining life

Having twins is hard work – it confronted me with all my inadequacies: I think too much; I procrastinate; I get too angry too quickly; I shout; I am frightened; I worry far too much what others think about everything; too often I sit and watch telly instead of doing the washing-up. I could go on. However, mostly I realised just how much I needed time doing nothing. Until I had children I had no idea how much I simply stared at the wall doing nothing. It was disguised as 'having a cup of tea' but was in fact 'me maintaining my mental well-being'. Without it I struggled.

Now, it should perhaps be acknowledged that this was all happening against a backdrop of all sorts of other difficult work, family and life events. Having children was by no means the only stressful event at this time – there were many things over which I was falling apart. But having children was one of the most personally confronting. It was also what pushed me out of my usual coping mechanisms and forced me to examine everything again, including how I understand and relate to my spirituality.

I already knew that my own family's mental health was not good, and in my mind connected with that was the knowledge that my grasp of 'God' was at best a tenuous one. When things are difficult for me I do not feel held and comforted. I feel alone and isolated. 'God' for me is not a 'hold-me-tight' feeling – it is not a secure thing. Before I had children I had thought about the idea that a human embryo grows within the context of a bigger living being and is born into her arms. For better or worse we are all nurtured from our very beginning within the love of another. I had wondered how then we could escape the concept of 'God', and I knitted attachment theory into my understanding of spirituality. I believed it was the destiny of people to search for the perfect parent – to search again for the perfect heldness of the womb. So, now being a mother, I related directly to Yahweh. The loneliness of being God. The responsibility. The fierceness of the love. The deepness of the fury. The sadness when I looked around the broken world and then back to my beautiful children. The Old Testament spoke to me of the mother I was – and I was cast in the role of God. No longer could I stand on the sidelines being the opinionated campaigner. I was now the protagonist, and, as with much of life, this is more difficult than it looks.

My church commitment amounted to sitting at the back of Quaker meeting on an irregular basis. I had been doing this for a number of years. Having children forced me to discuss with my husband what our church commitment might be. When we had first met we both worked within church contexts full time. Now, eight years on, he had no work or personal connections with his church and felt better for it. On the other hand, I, who when we first met was much more critical of the church, was now feeling rather nostalgic for that with which I had previously struggled. I valued the rituals of Christmas and Easter, the language of justice and the person of Jesus. I was beginning to think that children might benefit from what church can offer. So I began to negotiate with him about how my now growing commitment to the Quakers could be integrated into our family life.

Alongside this my babies grew into toddlers and into children. They made the most enormous mess (creative and growth-full!) in my home. I struggled to keep the physical business of things together and just about managed to wash all the nappies and cook all the food. However, keep the house manageably tidy? No, I failed consistently, and it was stressful. So, concrete lesson number one which my children taught me and which I just about manage to do now that the two oldest are six years old is: 'maintenance'. Do a little often and things will tick over. Not perfect but good enough. Somehow this is also true for my spirituality. If I leave it for too long things get out of hand. I begin to lose sense of where I am and what I need. So, committing to the Quakers, which was initially about what the children needed, has become very much something for me. I joined the Society of Friends and in the joining committed myself to attending regularly, being held accountable, giving money to support the work, taking responsibility for the running of the organisation and its global work. Maintenance.

The second thing which my children have taught me and which is transforming of the bit of me which wants to sit and stare at the wall is: 'live'! Small children live *now*. Not worrying about what happened yesterday and not thinking about what will happen tomorrow. Seeking out experiences. Assuming that others will want to play too. Fairly oblivious of the impact they are having around them. So alongside the imperative to 'maintain' has also come the learning that there are times to put down the chore and play – rediscovering the splashing in puddles, drinking hot chocolate in the bath, looking at the beauty of a daisy, running headlong into the wind, feeling mud squelching in your hand. The business of connecting with the physicalness of life – and how the heat of my love fires for the child next to me as we do these ordinary extra-ordinary things together. In these moments I am alive, properly alive as I haven't been for years.

Ruth Clements McQuaid

Wide Compassion ...

... On how connecting our lives with the lives of children, learning from them compassion and sharing with them a compassion for 'the other', connects us with the life of the world as we reach, in our separateness and togetherness, for a deeper belonging in community.

Arms open wide

What does it mean to belong? To be held safely in the arms of one who loves beyond measure, unconditionally, fully? As I grew I tussled with those who held me, who made me safe. I stretched boundaries and marked out my territory, daring anyone to challenge my independence. Looking back I know I needed the safety of those arms open wide in order to move, even to flee from them. To push them away, I needed love to push against. I needed to know I was held in order to be freely un-held. The paradox of growing.

As a teenager our family was augmented, for 6 years, by the lives of four young children who joined us. I'm not sure I knew, in my head, what it meant to be a foster family, but I knew in my gut how it felt to have the glorious Elizabeth join us for four years, followed by three others. I knew the joy of 'new' brothers and sisters, the fun and the caring that we all entered into, the jokes, the new games. I also knew the confusion and the pain. What did it mean for each one of these four to join us for a while, knowing that they would then move on? Was this, more or less, unsettling in their lives? I remember one child pushing the limits of caring so much, speaking his truth to power in saying: 'It doesn't matter: *you* won't keep me anyway.'

Scroll forward 30 years, and at the age of nine our eldest daughter returned from her first school residential trip. We had missed her for sure. But there had been a sweetness about our loss. For while we missed her presence, her chatter and her wisdom, her absence allowed us to miss her in a new way, and revealed a different space for our other family relationships to grow. But the missing came back with a vengeance as we waited, where we always waited, at the end of the school day to greet our returning child. As she turned the corner, as she always does, to walk across the playground to our meeting place, as she always does, I saw her again for the first time. Trundling her suitcase behind her, weighed down with the paraphernalia of a whole two nights away, my child walked towards me. And in that instant, I felt a tug in my gut, as if the elastic holding us umbilically, invisibly together had reached the limit of its tautness and I was impelled to move – to run – towards her. Arms open wide. Regardless of any embarrassment I may have caused, to her, to myself or others, I ran the short distance to her and snatched her up in my arms.

Hearts haiku

Hearts beat together –
miracle umbilical
springs life between us.

And at that moment I understood how it will be to meet God face to face. Arms open wide, God will embrace me as her much-loved child, running to meet me, impelled to move towards me as I am towards her. I have less fear of dying now. I have less curiosity about heaven, for I have glimpsed it on earth. I now know in my heart that the welcome will be almost unbearably sweet.

Ruth Harvey

You were there, and I was here

Strange indeed to be driven round the nightmarish maze that is the streets of London by a son whom it seems only a few years ago you led by the hand. Or to see your children tour Australia, or do volunteer work in Tamil Nadu, or help run a hotel in Spain. So strange.

Every parent must share this sense of bewilderment when they see their children as fully independent, autonomous adults. And of course, underneath it all, the perennial nagging worries. Did I do right?

I have six children by my first marriage, all well grown up now, plus one with my present partner, so I am in a curious position as a parent. Second time round the mulberry bush, so to speak. Fortunately, my grown-up children dote on their new little brother, and he loves them to bits. And me? I get confused, sometimes.

When I look at my sons and daughters from my first marriage, I am struck by two contradictory things. Firstly, how alike they are in their shared sense of humour, the warmth of their support for each other, and the strength of their identity as family, and, paradoxically, how different they are.

Thus, two of my daughters are committed practising Catholics, the third is less attached to the Church. Of my sons, two are on a rather tortuous spiritual journey, while the third jogs along, so to speak.

So, to what extent is this all my doing? They each know me differently, encountering me in a unique way, not just as part of a corporate unit, the 'family'. And as my life had its ups and downs this must have resonated with them, at the deepest, unconscious level, and in a way unique to each one.

Their mother is a deeply committed Catholic, not of the old repressive clericalist school, but post-Vatican II, a liberal and tolerant, ecumenically minded Christian. And she has been consistent and constant in her Catholicism. I, on the other hand, have a rather more varied religious history. And, to tell the truth, there was a period in my life when my religious faith did not mean as much to me as it does now.

Over the years, through my involvement with various political parties, I have come to see that all ideology is, as Phil Berrigan says, 'an attempt to justify murder as a social instrument', and all human political constructs are fatally flawed by egoism and the desire for power. The primary temptation offered by the serpent in the Garden of Eden was power – to be like God. And this was the temptation repeated to Christ when he was taken to a mountaintop, shown the kingdoms of the world, and offered power over them all. But there is no salvation in politics: salvation lies beyond all human plans and programmes, because all these are fatally flawed.

As the years have passed, I have grown more and more to see that the heart and soul of what I live by is the reality of Christ; the actuality of his birth, death and resurrection. I now appreciate these as real concrete historical events. The Resurrection was not some kind of vague symbolic non-event, some metaphorical expression of Christian hope or brotherhood. It was an actual event, as real as my own birth and inevitable death. This reality was experienced by the Apostles, and they transmitted this knowledge and faith in the risen Christ to those they met, who gave it to those they met, and so on, through the ages.

So while I am as politically active and committed as ever, my action, and my life, is now much more firmly based on a specifically spiritual foundation, my Christian faith.

My children have been the unwitting companions on my journey through life – with all my faults and failings. And regrets. 'I Did it My Way' could never be my party piece, because there is indeed much about my life that I regret. But we are born to learn, even if the learning is late in life.

And I have learnt much from my children. (Who was the famous philosopher who said: 'Whenever I have a really difficult question, I ask my seven-year-old daughter'?) Children have a directness that sees the basic simplicity of essential truth.

It must be going on 40 years ago that we were travelling north from the south of England. This was pre-motorway days, and we were travelling along a quiet, hedge-lined road. Eventually we spotted a wide grassy verge, where we pulled up, spread out the rug, and started to feed two small and very hungry children. At this point an irate female came bearing down on us like a galleon in full sail. 'This is my land! You can't stop here. You'll have to move on. This is my land!' And so on. So without a word, we packed up and drove on. After about ten minutes of silence, I heard a wee voice from the back of the car.

'Dad?'

'Yes?' I replied.

'That woman said that the land was hers. But it isn't her land. It's God's land.' …

There are so many such memories: Helen, aged 6, when we had moved to a new house in Caldercruix, and every book I had was temporarily stored in the garage, passing them through the window of the house to me so that I could stack them up indoors. Just a little girl, so eager to help her daddy.

And Peter, son number two, making his first communion: walking down the aisle in his suit, holding a carnation. But the head of the carnation had been knocked off, he was left holding a bare stem, and his wee lip was trembling …

Andrew, my youngest boy, and Peter singing out loudly and happily in the morning, from their bedroom next to ours – so full of the joys of life. 'Michael, Row the Boat Ashore'. A regular dawn chorus, welcoming a brand-new day.

Anna and Catherine, the youngest two, sitting at either side of the dinner table. Mary, my wife, mildly scolding Catherine for some childish transgression, and Anna's head going slowly down and the tears falling, in silent sympathy with her little sister.

And now they are all grown up, and regularly presenting me with grandchildren. And I am continually amazed at how lovely they are; how well-integrated and balanced. I can only conclude that their mother is largely responsible for their beautiful development.

I might hope that this time round I will not make the mistakes that I made the first time but I am not too sure about this. I suspect that I will still display the same failings and inadequacies. The only specific difference is that this time I will more resolutely refrain from any physical punishment. Where with my first children, I might have occasionally resorted to a mild slap, I do not do this with Seonaidh at all. I now believe that inflicting corporal (or mental) pain is never right.

Of course the real difference is that then, when I was young, I saw myself as founding a dynasty, with decades ahead of me. Now I am acutely aware of the fact that my threescore and ten years span is rapidly nearing its end. Mortality is tapping me on the shoulder.

But the strange thing is that the heart does not grow old or weak; because never was spring more a joy than this spring, which may be my last – never beauty in flower or woman more lovely, or child more enchanting, than now, when I am approaching the time of farewell to all these wonderful gifts.

Some time ago I took Seonaidh, at the age of four, to Byres Road where we were running a CND stall. I parked him on a bench near the stall with my friends, and started leafleting. Then I crossed the road, and continued handing out leaflets, while keeping an eye on him. After half an hour or so, I could see his wee face was sad, so crossed back over to him. There were tears in his eyes. I asked him what was wrong. 'You were there, and I was here,' he said.

His words went straight through me. Their simplicity, and the immensity of the unconscious truth of which they spoke. 'You were there, and I was here.' All the hurt and pain, the misunderstanding and failures of human relationships are present is these simple words from the lips of a four-year-old.

These words bring not only illumination, but some sort of consolation too. Perhaps much of what secretly pains me, the regrets that haunt me, are soothed by considering their truth. That the things I regret were the result of being in a different place, at a different time. Either that, or mere foolishness.

Brian Quail

On the Victoria Line

She took a tumble on the Victoria Line,
my daughter damaged by a faulty gene.
She wasn't able to step firmly
from solid ground to moving stairs.
I, wrestling with too much luggage and worry,
was disabled too.

A stranger caught her –
Chinese ... smiling ... as I recall.
He waved at me as the escalator
carried me downwards, away,
helpless against the London commuters
surging, tumbling down towards the trains.
I waved back, thankful for his strong hand
holding my daughter safe in the crowd.
An act of kindness in the city –
two strangers met for a moment
and knew it.

Where does such goodness come from?
My daughter does not understand
her gift for bringing people together.

Bryan Owen

Adoption hope

(A sermon preached during a 'Service of Thanksgiving, Reconciliation and Hope for Everyone Involved in Adoption', on Mothering Sunday, 14th March 1999, in Coventry Cathedral)

My name is Donald. I was adopted in July 1939 when I was 4 months old. My younger adopted brother and I have been well blessed both in our adopting parents and through what has become a wonderful wider family. We were told, before commencing school, simply and lovingly that we were both adopted. There was no real information about our origins and for many, perhaps too many, years no more conversation. That is how it was then. It's different now and I am glad.

As with some of you, there have been fantasies and fears, imaginings that do not go away, and a questioning that increases.

Since 1992 I have lived with a serious spinal condition necessitating three major operations. A few years ago, during one of the long periods of convalescence, I made my decision to search for my birth mother. The inner and outer journeys were both exhilarating and terrifying. I learned that in the facing of fears some inner healing can come. With the help of others 'a fat file' was discovered, including correspondence from my birth mother. Months later, I learned that both parents were dead.

Among us today are birth mothers, perhaps birth fathers, adopting parents, adopted people and family and friends who live with the implications of adoption. Each story is different. What brought us here is different.

Most of us, however, have at least one thing in common. We struggle for words to describe our complex inner world. Sometimes it feels like an underground river flowing within us, currents and whirlpools drawing us into places we'd prefer not to go, and shaping us in ways that we don't yet understand.

Most of us have never attended an occasion such as this. That is so for me too. This is the first time I have ever been asked to find words that can be said in public addressing what lies at the core of our experience as people living with the implications of adoption.

I am learning that there are painful yet wondrous gifts to be received through the adoption process, and I want to risk beginning to explore two particular areas, hoping there will be some echoes in your experience.

First, I want to speak of 'living with not knowing'. Understandably most of us still find it very hard to receive and to accept 'not knowing' as an unwelcome yet profound gift. At the core of my existence there lies what I can only call 'a dark hole of unknowing', and yet within the unknowing, a knowing. And this is not easily explained!

Each of us has lived with 'not knowing':

Where, among all the faces in a too crowded world, is the face of the person once carried in the womb, the one entrusted into the hands of others? And how can the silence and aloneness of 'not knowing' continue to be borne?

And who is this child, the child entrusted to adopting parents – the loved child – 'our child and yet not our child'?

And who is my mother? What pressures within circumstances made it necessary for her to give away her child? And where is she now?

And who is my father, lost in the shadows but growing in significance?

Most of us find it hard to live with the bewildering gift of 'not knowing'. There is a deep longing to know and yet also a terror of what may be found, of what could be made known. We want answers for our questions, deliverance from our continuing anguish, and help to live within the realities of our common human flawedness. And yet this untidiness, this incompleteness, this uncertainty, is how it is. And not for us alone.

And I wonder if there are some questions that must remain questions, some secrets that can remain hidden, some knowing that we don't need to know, and somehow, someday we may learn to live with them! Rainer Maria Rilke writes: *'Be patient toward all that is unsolved in your heart and try to love the questions themselves. Do not now seek the answers which cannot be given you because you would not be able to live them. And the point is, to live everything. Live the questions now.'*[1]

Perhaps 'the sense of mystery' lying at the heart both of human experience and of creation could become one of those painful and wondrous gifts we inherit? Michael Mayne, the former Dean of Westminster Abbey, writes: *'Faith is not about absolute certainty, but a readiness to explore mystery. It is not a method of finding all the answers, but of living with the questions.'*

And yet some of you know, as I now know too, some inner healing can only come through our searching, an endless exhausting searching through records, a searching through fearsome terrains in human experience, a searching within the strange synchronicity of time for a knowing that mysteriously makes itself known.

For me the most profound gift of living with 'not knowing' has been to enter the paradox of the unknowable God whose nature it is to continue to make himself known within life and through love – a knowing within an unknowing.

And secondly, I want to speak about 'the holding'. Most of us, I guess, are still on the edge of what 'the holding' can mean. There is, I am learning, 'a holding' that engenders a trusting, and a trusting that permits a letting go.

Can words ever tell what it means for a birth mother to hold her child, to hold and to trust, to let go and to entrust, to let go and yet to continue to hold in the inner cave of her being – a letting go that is not a forgetting but rather a different way of holding?

Can words ever tell what it means for adopting parents to hold and to nurture the child they receive, the child whose nature, whose genes they do not share? A holding and watching over growing adopted children who can be so different, in appearance, in temperament, in the worlds they choose to inhabit, so different, yet sometimes knowing a bonding that is closer than blood. A holding and trusting in such a way that one day a new letting go becomes possible, the entrusted one let go again, an essential letting go that alone permits the returning, but a returning in a different way.

Can words ever tell what it is for those of us who are adopted to be held and not controlled, to be influenced in the process of becoming who we are, influenced but not twisted and shaped into the likeness of someone we cannot be, searching for roots within our unrootedness, for belonging within our aloneness?

Can words ever tell what it is to learn the holding of our complex inner world, the wild and sullen bits that sometimes take over, the inner feelings for which we have no names, the bottomless sorrow, the unshed tears and the overwhelming rage?

Slowly I am learning that there is 'a holding' that befriends and integrates, embraces and pays attention to those bits of us that we fear and from which we hide – a holding that, in time, can release a wondrous healing.

I am holding in my hand a beautiful piece of wood carved into the shape of a cross by an old man in West Bromwich. Sometimes these little pieces of wood are offered to those who are dying, people for whom words cease to carry meaning, people who find the letting go much harder than they thought. For some these little pieces of wood become alive, calming wild dreams and those long dark nights when we wait for the dawn.

For some these small wooden crosses draw them into a mystery, the mystery of 'the holding' of God, 'the holding' through the trauma of being born through the trauma of dying. There is a short and ancient prayer: 'I hold and am held'. It bears testimony to the hidden holding of God's love within the texture of our fragility and fragmentation.

I have spoken of two things: learning to 'live with not knowing' and of 'the holding and being held'. Both, I believe, can be the painful and wondrous gifts for those who live within the adoption process. And not for us alone!

Donald Eadie

Notes:

1. From Letter Four, 23rd April, 1903, in *Letters to a Young Poet*, Rainer Maria Rilke, first published in 1934 in English by W.W. Norton and Co of New York, and in 1929 in German as *Briefe an Einen Jungen Dichter* in Leipzig by Insel-Verlag. Now published in 2011 by Penguin Classics of Harmondsworth, and translated by C. Louth

Family photograph

Yo-ho, Tommy Sandy! How are things over there?
I think of you from time to time.
Do you sink the odd pint? I like a drink too.
Do you still play cribbage? Not letting me win
I expect was good for my soul.
All the others were easy on me, back then.
This is the fate of only-children, a soft living,
then smack against the wall. Oh, the pain!
You have to bide your time until you're grown up,
grown up and strong, the way you are in this picture.
Tommy, I have your cuff links.

I keep them in a box marked G. Browne of Bingley
– All Kinds of Watches and Jewellery Repaired –
along with my other Grandad's bowling medal.
Imagine being Champion of the whole of Glasgow.
The bird that never flew. The tree that never grew.
They placed the coat of arms on top of a Saltire.
Imagine baptising me into the English Church!
I'm as Scottish as whisky and freedom.
I know you're from Grimsby.
Up the Mariners!

I'm looking at you in about 1925.
This is before Elsie was born.
Grandma Ada has Annie on her knee. Annie has your dimple.
Aunt Nell and Mum have floppy ribbons in their hair.
Nell with her huge smile, Mum quiet and thoughtful.
Believe me, Tommy: they never changed.
You know I envy you all this.
In our family we only knew the wee one as Annie, who died.
That was her name to us, Annie-who-died.
So what's it like now? I mean you're all five together.
Elsie thinks of you too.

Do you know she has a granddaughter in Surrey?
She says things like: Grandma, I really love you,
but you do talk funny. Ho!

What if she could remember you the way I do,
the horse brasses, the mantelshelf with all its doohickeys,
the garden with its strawberry nets and roses?
What would she make of those flat Yorkshire vowels?
Eeeehhhhh!
Grandad, I really love you but you do talk funny.
What would she think of her cousins in Aberdeenshire?
I think her name is Emily, but then again
maybe it's Charlotte.

How are you getting on with Dad?
Does he still think Communism is the answer?
Do he and Mum ever walk hand in hand?
Do they hold hands at all?
As far as I know they never did back here.
He just banged on about politics.
I mean, from youth until the day he died.
One way, there's only one way.
It must feel good to be so secure in your faith.
Of course he hated all forms of dogma.
Listen Tommy, rather you than me!

I can't say it's all been good since you went.
We've had our share of suicides and sad endings.
Things haven't turned out too well, not that it's finished.
I'm on my own now. Nice flat but – you know.
I have a woman friend who stays over, sometimes.
I won't go into that. Mum hated all that part of my life.
Listen, if you have any influence over there,
would you mind distracting her at such times?
You'll know when. I'd really appreciate it.
Do you understand this is the middle of the night
I'm speaking from?

I'm looking at the photo again. You're maybe thirty-three.
Not a big guy. That comes down the female side.
How long did you have with Grandma Ada?
Twelve years? Were you happy, Tommy?
Did you make her happy? Did she you?
One stepdaughter, three daughters of your own.

Two deaths. First Annie, then Ada.
Back then it could have been worse.
That chain across your waistcoat has two dangly things.
One looks like a ring. What was that, Tommy?
What is it I know nothing of?

It looks like you've been lit from above.
The bottom half of the picture is all darkness.
Long lace-up boots, skirts, trousers, all dark;
the detail is going. I'm losing it from the bottom up.
There's a certain amount of background fading too.
Your eyes look out from under the shadow of your brow.
Seen this way, they bespeak the terrible intensity
I thought came down just from Dad.
But you're happy, aren't you?
It's there at the corners of your mouth.

You look so proud of your family, respectable and strong.
It's good to see you looking substantial.
If only we could shake hands, Tommy.
You look good too, in that sharp wool jacket.
Light fawn must have been pretty daring back then.
I notice your bow tie is a shiny satin job, your wing collar
in plain white contrast to your fancy shirt front.
Do you know what I'd like?
I'd like you to step out of the picture, on to the desk.
I'd like it if you could walk around the cuff links.
Go on, push them about a bit with your foot.
I'd like it if you could wave, wink from the picture, speak
with your own voice. Something.

Robert Davidson

Caring for Elizabeth

For about seven years in the late 1970s and early 1980s, our family was involved in a Barnardo's fostering scheme for hard-to-place children. This was a groundbreaking scheme at the time, and it was a privilege to be part of it. The objective was to take hard-to-place and vulnerable children, place them with foster parents for between a year and three years, with the hope that at the end of that time they would move into permanent adoptive families. For a year beforehand, we joined with the other potential foster parents in training – two hours every fortnight. During our time as part of the scheme, as well as continuing to meet every fortnight with the other foster parents, we had personal social work support from Barnardo's, and of course the children whom we were fostering had their own social worker. It was an extremely well-run scheme; and we were paid a professional fee.

Our first foster child, who was with us for nearly three years, was a lovely five-year-old girl who had suffered brain damage at birth. In the event, Elizabeth did not find a permanent adoptive family; but what she did find was a wonderful long-term foster family, with whom, as far as we know, she lives still.

Elizabeth was a huge challenge in many ways. The event I want to share took place quite early during her time with us. I should say that at that time, I was serving as parish minister of a housing scheme parish in Stirling. This particular week, I had just been involved in a harrowing pastoral situation. An older woman in our congregation had received devastating news from her son, serving as a policeman in the Royal Ulster Constabulary (as it was then called) in Northern Ireland. His teenage daughter, her granddaughter, a bright and normally cheerful young girl, had latterly become very depressed about the situation in Belfast during 'the Troubles'. Earlier that week, while her parents were out shopping, she had apparently gone into her father's room, found his police revolver, and shot herself – dead. You can imagine the devastation of that whole family – not least of the grandmother in Stirling.

A day or so after that event, a formal 'case conference' for Elizabeth was held in our manse. I can't be sure now – but I think there must have been at least ten, if not more, professional people gathered in our living room. Doctors, teachers, psychiatrists, social workers, Barnardo's staff and ourselves – there we all were, pooling what must have been quite an impressive amount of hard-earned experience and knowledge … all in an effort to help one severely damaged child.

I remember being struck at the time by the huge contrast between the situations of the two girls. On the one hand, a teenager, with so much going for her, yet feeling so isolated, and so defeated, that she was driven to take her own life. And on the other hand, a little girl, with perhaps a mental age of one and a half, with hardly any prospects at all – yet the object of so much detailed and highly skilled care and attention.

Two things about these two contrasting situations struck me then – and strike me still.

There is the fact that all children can be so utterly, utterly vulnerable. I knew that, of course – but the impact of the stories of these two young girls on my life in that one week made it real in a way which had never quite happened before.

But I was also left with mixed emotions. The tragedy of the teenager in Northern Ireland left me feeling very angry and very helpless – angry at the way children sometimes have to pay so dearly for the failure of adults and the adult world, and helpless before the seeming intractability of the situation. Yet the presence of all these professionals in our house, gathered round what some might have been tempted to write off as a 'hopeless case', made me feel proud to belong to a society that could enable that sort of event to take place.

John Harvey

Forgiveness

'We have to forgive our parents for the wrongs they unwittingly committed against us. Only then can we ask our children to forgive us for the wrongs we have unwittingly committed against them' – a quote from a wise woman friend of ours, which we had on our kitchen door for many years until it was lost in a 'flitting' (move). We never actually made a conscious decision to have an 'open door' sort of lifestyle. It just gradually evolved and became a way of life. Over the years we did, at various points, wonder about the impact of this on our own children, and we tried to rebalance it when we felt it necessary – sometimes more successfully than others.

The conscious decision to foster through an innovative Barnardo's project was, however, just that – a conscious decision. It came about because we were in a position where I needed to supplement the family income, while at the same time I didn't want to work outside the home. This Barnardo's project seemed to be the answer: we were to be paid a salary for fostering vulnerable children with a view to preparing them for adoption. So I could contribute to the family income without working outside the family home. With the benefit of hindsight it's easy to see that this may not have been the best thing for our children. Maybe it would have been better to have had a 9 to 5 job outside the home in order to be more available for our children.

Our children, over the years, often had to take second place to needy people who were around our home. Again with hindsight we can look back and say: Did we, because of this lifestyle, fail our own children? This is a sobering and very scary thought.

'Good enough' parenting was what we always hoped we were doing. My sincere hope and prayer now is that this was in fact the case.

Molly Harvey

Marian

Bring me a rocking chair –
and bring me all the unrocked babies plunged
so savagely from light to darkness;
that I may rock them, sing to them,
and weave for them a thread of tenderness
which they may cling to when no longer babes,
in all the harshnesses about them and
show gentleness, remembering gentleness.

This poem was written by my mother and reflects the longing I had to bring care to neglected children. I only succeeded with one. In the worst orphanage in Vietnam in which our Quaker team worked, there was a wee tadpole of a child who lifted up her arms to me as I passed her cot. It was love at first sight.

Marian, named after my mother, was a child of the Vietnam War. She hadn't even a birth certificate because her original orphanage was raided during the night and the children scattered to several orphanages. One of thirty children in cots in a large room, she lay totally neglected.

Because, at 32, I was pretty sure I wouldn't have a child of my own, I adopted Marian. I asked Helen from our volunteer group to be her godmother. Fortunately, she consented.

Marian was always a self-possessed child, never complaining, eager to please. She could play for hours with two Lego bricks. Because of her early malnutrition, Marian had a compulsive appetite. While in California awaiting the completed adoption, we stayed with my cousin, and ate our meals at her 'bar' on tall stools. Marian's first meal there consisted of rice. When she dropped two grains on the floor, she laboriously climbed down from the stool to retrieve them!

On arriving in California, when she was three, Marian had been so disadvantaged in the orphanage that she was neither toilet-trained, nor could she walk. But because I had to get a job immediately, and she had to go into a nursery, she quickly perceived the need for these skills – and acquired them!

The only time I remember Marian being really frightened was when, in Penpont, Dumfriesshire, she heard her first low-flying plane there. She screamed in terror: She remembered.

Possibly the plunge into an English-speaking environment from a Vietnamese one contributed to Marian's early lack of language. But her intuition emerged in other ways. She always loved Wild Goose songs, and was always re-recording them. Surprisingly, one of the darker songs about torture and death, taught to us at Peace House by Maggie Hamilton, became her first choice among many.

The year of the adoption, 1974-75, was the most difficult year of my life. I found Californian lifestyle untenable and longed for my dear Quaker friends in London. In 1976 Helen and her housemate invited us to share their house in Dumfriesshire. When Helen was appointed Justice and Peace worker for the Iona Community we moved to Dunblane, where we started Peace House. There Marian started attending the Rudolf Steiner school Ochil Tower, in Auchterarder, where she was helped to express herself non-verbally. We still have her lovely painting of a candle, and the rough wooden spoon and bird box that she made.

Until 2000 Marian was happy to participate in peace demonstrations, and to help as much as possible with Peace House. The fact that since then she has distanced herself from the peace movement is possibly to do with her fears and memories of war and its effects. I suspect this is why she has remained more in her imagination, yet facing all occasions with equanimity. After all as an infant in Vietnam she experienced unspeakable destruction.

Ellen Moxley

A song for Marian

Marian quietly watching the world
So much within that's yet to unfurl
Glimpses you give of the treasure within
So good and lovely you are.

Such a joy to be having around
Peace and gentleness in you are found
Sharing, caring and giving so much
Our hearts you tenderly touch.

Marian coming to brighten our dark
Lighting our lives with your symbol of hope
Showing in drawings your care for us all
So good and lovely you are.

Delighting in music, rejoicing in sound
The pleasure you give us is not often found
The smile in your eyes, your laugh in our ears
Brings happiness to our days.

Marian, you who have so much to love
Marian, you who have so much to give
Filling our lives with your joy and your peace
So good and lovely you are.

Judith Driver

A Letter to Ella from Apse* (Grandfather) on your Blessing Day

20th January, 2008

Dear Ella,

Today, surrounded by many who love you dearly, you were blessed in Christ's name. With or without a blessing, you are God's child and carry within you the image of the One who created you. I hope you will always treasure that great truth. Your blessing confirms this in a special way. The famous German theologian Hans Kung, who is still very much alive, reminded us many years ago that to be 'in Christ' is to know what it is to be 'fully human'. I hope you will always be a rich, open, self-aware human being – with a sense of humour and the ability to see your own craziness! I love that insight that we have to take the world seriously, and God seriously, but our own selves more lightly.

When your mum and dad told me about your blessing, I thought about the rich Christian heritage which you have from both sides of your family. For many years I worked on the tiny island of Iona off the west coast of Scotland. Away back in the 6th century, Saint Columba and his monks set up their monastery on Iona and shared the Good News of the Gospel all over the land. They even went as far as modern Russia and Turkey, enduring many hardships along the way, to tell people about Jesus. It may be, Ella, that our own Christian faith (yours and mine) goes right back to these Celtic monks who lived more than fifteen hundred years ago. A wonderful thought! And today all over the world, there are millions of others, tens of millions, who, along with your family, walk on the path of Jesus. That fact came home to me again very strongly a few weeks ago when I was in Palestine – the country where Jesus was born and carried out his ministry.

Of course I would like you one day to see yourself as a committed follower of Christ in our fragile but still beautiful world. A world filled with both laughter and tears. But if you do become a follower of Christ, I hope it will open your heart more and more to the cries of the world and to the cries of our earth – that good earth upon which we all walk and which sustains us each day, and which today is so deeply wounded.

As a theologian, I find it difficult to accept any form of Christianity which is solely concerned about keeping our own lives comfortable. How can we be comfortable, Ella, in a world in which two thirds of the human race live on less than a dollar a day? We cannot be. Jesus has taught us that we are all connected as sisters and brothers on this small planet, and He constantly calls us to work for peace, for lasting justice and to the care of creation itself. All of us are just on earth for a very short time, even if you live to be 100, but in that short time we can live with awareness, with compassion and with a deep integrity of spirit. I hope that people will be able to say of you in future that you are an inspirational person who accepts people in all of their extraordinary diversity, hope and vulnerability. And you don't need to be rich, nor powerful to be such a person.

You will soon learn that we live in violent times. There are wars and rumours of wars in many parts of our interconnected world. Terrible poverty touches into the lives of billions of people. Sadly, although true, one of the causes of these wars is religion. So my hope is (my prayer is) that you will always be open to those who walk on a path other than Christian. May you be able to see the beauty and wisdom and truth in other cultures, traditions and faiths, while remaining true to your own understanding. There is no place in our world for religious intolerance, which is why it is crucial for you to embrace both cultural and human diversity in love. I love the prayer which says: 'Stay with us, Lord, for the day is far spent and we have not yet recognised Your face in each of our sisters and brothers.' Without this wide compassion, the world in which you are growing up will only become a place rent asunder more and more by war, famine and increasing injustice. Never make your God too small or too domesticated.

My prayer for you today (and I am sure the prayer of all of us who love you) is that you will in your own life always reflect something of the light, compassion and wisdom of the One who came to this earth to bring us all new life and healing and love. In my own life, despite many failings and false starts and wrong turnings, I deeply believe that Jesus Christ brought these things and many more to our world, and I hope that one day you will believe that too. A great man called Saint Augustine once said a beautiful thing: 'Our hearts are restless till they find their rest in God.' His words are perhaps even more true today than when he wrote them many centuries ago.

You are blessed in Christ, Ella, and you have already brought many blessings to others even though you will be only three in March. That is just wonderful – a small miracle in fact. Or maybe a big one!

Hundreds of years before you came into the world, a good and holy person living in the Highlands of Scotland wrote a prayer which has been loved by millions of people ever since. It is very simple, but also very powerful. It's my prayer for you today – on this day of your blessing:

> *May the raindrops fall lightly on your brow,*
> *may the soft winds freshen your spirit,*
> *may the sunshine brighten your heart,*
> *may the burdens of the day rest lightly upon you,*
> *and may God enfold you in the mantle of his love.*

With lots and lots of love,
your Apse x

*Apse – a family 'nickname'

Peter Millar

A community of families

We are two friends with children of similar ages who live close to each other. When our children were babies, we often talked about how, whilst nothing had prepared us for the overwhelming joy and happiness brought by our children, at the same time nothing had prepared us for the extremes of tiredness and the sometimes negative feelings of angst and frustration. We found this not only physically and emotionally challenging, but spiritually too. Bearing these challenges in mind, and keen to nurture our children in a Christian context, we started to take practical and deliberate steps to bring some spiritual meaning to our children's lives, while sustaining and growing our own faith at the same time.

There is an African saying: 'It takes a whole village to raise a child.' While we haven't embraced fully the multi-generational aspect of this ethos, we have sought to be a community of families at a similar life stage. Some of what we have done has left us with a feeling of accomplishment, some has left us worn out, but the effort seems worth it. Not only are we sharing the stresses of having young families, we are also seeking to provide our children with a living spirituality which will shape their lives and give them roots. We have deliberately introduced symbolism and ritual into family life through fun activities and eating together. We hope this will form memories they can draw on as they grow up and decide what shape their own lives will take. We have chosen to use some of the ideas and traditions of the millions who have gone before us as Christians, as well as some of our own, to bring a sense of spirituality to the ordinariness of life.

Life is busy, and extra meetings can bring a sense of tiredness and failure to hard-working parents. Doing things on an irregular or spontaneous basis has worked well for us and meant that we don't feel pressure or guilt when something doesn't happen. A day out, a cup of tea or a meal together is achievable. We have sometimes planned more structured activities and invited others. Inviting friends to church isn't always easy, but inviting families to make some Advent biscuits and listen to a story together seems to work. Our activities have ranged from making wooden crosses in the garden on Good Friday (not sure what the neighbours thought), to a Halloween mystery trail and 'back to school' prayer activities on the Humber foreshore. Children are naturally curious in asking questions about life and about God. We have tried to help them find a language to express those questions, and to explore ways of worshipping and praying in the ordinary.

We have found that looking after ourselves and our adult friendships has been as important as doing things with the children. Sunday night 'chats' over a glass of wine, or going for a walk or a swim (when we have had the energy) have kept us going. A 'Mum's escape' to Camas, the Iona Community's outdoor centre on Mull, for a week was very special and something we will always remember. Food has also been an important part of our journey! Perhaps our most successful and rewarding venture has been our weekly meal swap. For the past few years we have made a 'meal for 2' for each other one night a week. Not culinary competition but simple food which has been fun and easy to give. Making extra food to give has required little thought or effort. Receiving a meal once a week is a real treat and we and our partners all look forward to 'our night' for a food delivery!

As life has moved on and we have said goodbye to the 'nappy days' (hooray), we have tried to adapt to our families' changing needs. Our 9+-year-old boys tell us that sometimes 'Church is boring', but that they still want to think about God. Thus a small group of self-named 'one-eyed ninjas' have started meeting on Friday nights for activities mainly social and occasionally thoughtful. We hope this will be a time when they can build relationships, but also feel safe to carry on thinking and asking questions too.

We hope to continue journeying together. We know that, whatever life brings, we will have some great memories and firm friendships to sustain us in the future.

Ros Davies and Liane Kensett

Parenting as vocation

Parenthood has not been the path I expected. Having my first child at 18 shaped my whole life. In many ways my eldest daughter has had the most and the worst of me. It was just the two of us for ages, yet I was young and careless, too. Having the chance to have a second family ten years later, when I was experienced as a child psychologist, was very humbling, and I tried to do better. Then along came two more babies in quick succession and all my ideals were shelved as we simply struggled to get through each day. Sometimes we argued as a family – me and my new partner and my daughter – and it was like a part of my soul being split off. Yet we worked hard at reconciliation, and still do.

Being a parent and being a spiritual person are somewhat difficult to disengage for me, because I have been a parent for all of my adult life and because each time I have become a parent of someone new it has been a deeply spiritual experience that has felt like an incredibly humbling taste of the creativity which must constantly excite God.

My children have brought me closer to God, enriching my life immeasurably and it often feels as though they have taught me far more than I could offer any of them. I have not always been a good parent, yet I have been forgiven by them more readily than by myself. And I have been loved by them far more than I feel my narrow heart offers. These sentiments are so similar to how I feel about my relationship with God that I suppose just being with the children is a spiritual experience.

Yet this great privilege comes with responsibility, just like the road of Christian discipleship. I feel that it is important to give myself up to my children when they really need me, and this is something that my partner and I have agreed between us is necessary for us as parents. So we hold the children and their needs, as far as we can, at the centre of our shared lives and have tried to fit in other things around them. This has meant many sacrifices, exhaustion, and at times financial hardship and having no life beyond our home. Yet we believe the benefits for the children and the family as a whole of having us around when they are small, and not using childcare until it is an opportunity for the children (instead of a convenience for us), are irreplaceable.

There are many things we don't have, yet by not having them we seem to have gained so much. The six of us live in a lovely basement flat, but have no garden, so we share two allotments with friends with children the same age – a far more enriching, community- and wildlife-oriented experience than having our own garden – and we have all enjoyed it so much! Similarly, the three little ones all share a room, partitioned off our bedroom, yet their ability to co-operate and share with one another is amazing, and a continual discipline. Sometimes in the middle of the night we find one in bed with another, screaming loudly while the other sleeps!

Being a parent stretches me to my very limit, and is always a place of succour and challenge. It is both my learning edge and my safe haven. Again, this is very like my sense of God. It is as if, through all my life, God has been in and with and alongside this hugely important, highly skilled and terribly undervalued job, teaching me about myself and showing me how to give of myself to the people on whom I will have the most impact my life long.

And the path of parenting is so similar to the path of discipleship: self-sacrifice, discipline, love, joy, far more coming back than is ever given out, learning, growth and challenge, repeated failure, and repeated forgiveness and hope. Perhaps it is a vocation after all.

Elizabeth Wild

Bibliography and Resources

The books and resources listed below were all suggested, in connection with the themes of this book, by the contributors to this collection. If they have given a reason for their choice this has been included in quotes after the reference, with their name at the end. If they gave no comment, their name is simply listed in brackets after the reference.

A Man for All Seasons (film and book): 'Essential to "walk the talk"' (Ellen Moxley)

'Ah, Sweet Mystery of Life' (song): 'Because, as my father was dying, he said to my mother: *It's true, just like the old song says: 'Tis love and love alone the world is seeking ... 'tis the answer, 'tis the end and all of living. For it is love alone that rules for aye!* And this is true. But love is a heavy cross.' (Brian Quail)

Alice in Wonderland, Lewis Carroll (Neil Paynter)

Alligator Pie, Dennis Lee: 'Excellent children's poetry' (Neil Paynter)

Big Mama Makes the World, Phyllis Root and Helen Oxenbury: 'Re-telling of the creation story with God as an Afro-Caribbean mum. I love an alternative image of God presented to children – shows that a variety of images of God exist and are helpful. This book has beautiful pictures, and will always hold happy memories of bedtime stories with my daughters.' (Rachael Yates)

Caring for Planet Earth, Ian M. Fraser: 'We discovered this little book by chance and have greatly enjoyed it. It has a similar layout to Nancy Cocks' book (see *Growing Up with God*), with a story, a prayer and a reflection – providing great material for a discussion. The main idea is for children to be aware of their environment and our planet and to know that there are ways of justice and peace to help life on earth. (Lucie Miller)

Coming Home to Self: Healing the Primal Wound, Nancy Verrier: 'A book that enables positive and honest reflection within our various stages of growing into whatever maturity might mean!' (Donald Eadie)

Creative Arts Therapies (including drama, play, art and sculpture): 'I loved learning about these ideas and then bringing them home to use in play with my eldest daughter. She vividly remembers them!' (Elizabeth Wild)

Dead Poets Society (film): 'Was inspirational when I was beginning my teaching career, encouraging teachers to think outside the box.' (Shirley Billes)

Dibs in Search of Self, Virginia M. Axline (Ruth Clements McQuaid)

Elizabeth Joy: A Mother's Story, Caroline Philps, 'Caroline Philps struggles with the same questions of faith and doubt I wrestled with when Catriona was born with Down's Syndrome.' (Katy Owen)

Gently Lead: How to Teach Your Children about God While Finding Out for Yourself, Polly Berrien Berends: 'This book helped me when I needed to actually nourish my own spiritual growth.' (Suzanne Swanson)

Growing up with God, Nancy Cocks: 'This is a tremendous book which is a great resource for a family discussion on very common life situations in a Christian context.' www.ionabooks.com (Lucie Miller)

Hugo and Josephine, Maria Gripe: 'Life through the eyes of two children' (Ellen Moxley)

I and Thou, Martin Buber: 'This book shines with the primacy of relationship.' (Ellen Moxley)

Ignatian Exercises in Daily life: 'I did a "Growth in Prayer and Reflective Living" course first, then the "Retreat in Daily Life" over 9 months. This gave me tools to reflect on daily life, to find God in the ordinary small things – so important for a mum – to rediscover God as vibrant, creative and present in my life.' (Rachael Yates)

In a Dark Time, Robert J. Lifton and Nicholas Humphrey: 'The need to live hopefully' (Ellen Moxley)

Lego and Playmobil: 'Hours spent in play with children who can lose themselves in stories and imagination.' (Lis Mullen)

Lord of the Flies, William Golding: 'This explores the negative, dark side of human nature, as revealed in children.' (Brian Quail)

Motherhood and God, Margaret Hebblethwaite: 'Helped me see my experience as a mother as a way to incorporate spirituality into daily life, instead of finding motherhood a "barrier" to living my spiritual life.' (Rachael Yates)

Mummy, Why Have I Got Down's Syndrome?, Caroline Philps and Pat Alexander: 'Caroline Philps crystallises the joys and dilemmas facing parents with Down's children.' (Katy Owen)

Norah Jones, Santana, The Red Hot Chili Peppers, The Foo Fighters, Christy Moore and countless others: 'Great music to give birth to, dance with in labour, and enjoy with small people when they are grown.' (Elizabeth Wild)

Parent as Mystic, Mystic as Parent, David Spangler: 'I enjoyed this book because it looked at parenting from the perspective of spirituality.' (Elizabeth Wild)

Prayer Rhythms for Busy People, Ray Simpson (Ros Davies and Liane Kensett)

Quaker Faith and Practice (Ruth Clements McQuaid)

Sleeping with Bread: Holding What Gives You Life, Dennis Linn, Sheila Fabricant Linn and Matthew Linn: 'This book has given us the basis for nightly prayer in our home, as we reflect on what gives us and what denies us life.' (Ruth Harvey)

Something More: Nurturing Your Child's Spiritual Growth, Jean Grasso Fitzpatrick (Suzanne Swanson)

Speaking of God: A Collection of Stories, Trevor Dennis (Ruth Clements McQuaid)

Stephen Fischbacher: 'Fischy music has touched children at their most joyful moments and at their points of hardest struggle. The songs affirm their life and faith experiences as well as being great fun!' www.fischy.com (Shirley Billes)

The Adoption Triangle, Julia Tugendhat: 'Essential reading for anyone concerned with adoption. This book helped me to value and begin to understand how it must be for a birth parent and adopting parents. Readable, understandable, wise and empathic.' (Donald Eadie)

The Children We Deserve: Love and Hate in the Making of the Family, Rosalind Miles (John and Molly Harvey)

The Church Calendar (Festivals and days of the Christian year) (Ros Davies and Liane Kensett)

The Enneagram: 'The Enneagram is a fascinating tool which has helped me to discover that we are all born looking at the world through a particular lens which affects the way we react to the world around us.' (Shirley Billes)

The Evil Eye of Gondôr, Bryan Owen: 'This is a play I wrote for children. It is a celebration of community.' (Bryan Owen)

The Little Prince, Antoine de Saint-Exupéry (Neil Paynter)

The Nation's Favourite Poems of Childhood (Bryan Owen)

The Primal Wound: Understanding the Adopted Child, Nancy Verrier: 'For the first time I began to find a language for an inner world I could not understand or explain.' (Donald Eadie)

The Spiritual Life of Children, Robert Coles: 'A refreshing book which comes out of the writer's experience of listening to children and his friendship with them.' (Ken Lawson)

'The Toys', Coventry Patmore, in *Life & Death: A Collection of Classic Poetry and Prose*, Philip Pullman: 'Because it expresses the pain of fatherhood, and relates this to God's attitude towards us.' (Brian Quail)

Transactional Analysis for Kids, Alvyn Freed: 'Helps understanding and communication between children and adults, giving a common language' (Ken Lawson)

What Is God Like?, Marie-Agnès Gaudrat and Ulises Wensell: 'Very simple language accompanied by gentle pictures of children's activities. This book is a wonderful resource because it portrays God and faith in simple but fundamental terms.' (Lucie Miller)

Wild Goose Songs: 'We all like to listen to Wild Goose music, to learn the tunes and sing along. The short, simple chants (usually from Africa) have been a great enrichment to our daily lives.' www.ionabooks.com (Lucie Miller)

Winnie the Pooh, A.A. Milne and Ernest Shepard: 'Accessible to all ages, giving some recognisable personalities and lovely humour' (Ken Lawson)

Woody Guthrie: 'These simple songs made us all happy, and helped us find the lightness and love in ordinary daily life.' (Suzanne Swanson)

Your Baby and Child, Penelope Leach: 'Lots of good common-sense advice' (Flo MacIntyre)

Contributors

Contributors were invited to share, along with a biography, a note of places that have inspired them as they have lived alongside children.

Shirley Billes: Born and brought up in the South side of Glasgow with my parents and sister. I left Jordanhill College with a Bachelor of Education degree in 1989 and became a primary teacher. I married Rolf Billes in July 1991 and spent a year living in Germany. After returning to Glasgow, where I continued teaching, we lived in Kilmarnock for five years where Rolf ministered in a housing scheme called Shortlees. During this time I became a full-time mum looking after our three beautiful daughters, Anna, Rachel and Katie. Sadly, I also suffered an early miscarriage in Kilmarnock. We named our heavenly baby Peter. We then moved to the parish of St Andrews Lhanbryd & Urquhart in Morayshire, where we had Molly, our fourth beautiful daughter. During the whole of our ministry together, I have enjoyed working with children and young people and writing worship material for use in church services and with small groups. After eight happy years in Moray, my family moved to the parish of Colinton, Edinburgh.

Places: Teaching in Drumchapel, Glasgow: Where I learned about working with vulnerable children and about the enduring ability of some parents to overcome very difficult circumstances for the sake of their children. Working with Yvonne McCorkindale, the children and youth worker in Shortlees: Yvonne and the children in Shortlees taught me much about compassion, patience and being flexible while sticking firmly to important boundaries. My present employment involves working in schools, alongside chaplains, around self-esteem issues, where I am reminded of the enormous enthusiasm which children bring to daily life. My home: Bringing up four children has taught me most about the pleasure and the pain involved in growing up. The privilege of parenting is something I will never take for granted.

Victoria Blease lives in Cumbria and loves her home and garden and nature's playground. She strives for a life of creativity and simplicity, when she isn't tripping up on Lego pieces.

Ruth Clements McQuaid grew up in Scotland believing she was English, only to go to England and to discover she was not English, but not quite Scottish either, thus throwing her into a search for a sense of belonging which is unfinished. Along the way she has enjoyed playing and listening to music, eating and drinking with good company, qualified and practised as a youth and community worker, married a lovely and long-suffering man, delivered and grappled with three growing children, and discovered that true happiness is surely camping on Mull.

Places: Kelvingrove Museum with my children; our tent and its surroundings; the allotment; Lincoln Cathedral

Robert Davidson has carried Iona and the Iona Community in his heart since first visiting in the 1960s. Since then he has become a writer, editor and publisher based in Highland Scotland. His latest book is *Site Works*, published by Sandstone Press.

Ros Davies: When I'm not doing 'family stuff', or spending time with friends, I work as a GP in Hull. I like cooking, crochet, swimming and learning to play the piano.

Places: Camas Adventure Centre, Isle of Mull; our home; our favourite days out, appealing to all ages, are Fountains Abbey and the Yorkshire Sculpture Park – both places where nature's beauty and human creativity meet to brilliant effect.

Donald Eadie is adopted. He lives in Moseley, a multicultural area in Birmingham, with his wife, Kerstin. He is a retired Methodist minister, formerly a Tutor in Pastoral Theology at Wesley College, Bristol and Chairman of the Birmingham District of the Methodist Church. For about 15 years he has lived with a serious spinal condition. Donald is now freer to be with people who also ponder life and its meaning, search for a fresh sense of direction and wonder what God is up to in all this. Donald and Kerstin are parents of two daughters and have five grandchildren.

Places: Our family owns a simple wooden cottage by a lake in the forests of central Sweden. Our daughters and their families love being there. We watch the fish jump, the birds swoop, the elk hovering by the roadside. It is a place for being, wondering and gazing. I take our grandchildren to Edgbaston Cricket Ground for one-day games and we get excited together. I belong to the back row at church: some call us crocks' corner because we are in wheelchairs and special chairs. We love to watch and chat with the children as they come in and out of church. They inspire us.

Joyce Gunn Cairns is a professional artist, living and working in Edinburgh. For information on her work visit www.joycegunncairns.co.uk

John and Molly Harvey: Sole qualification for contributing to this book is the life-enhancing and utterly amazing experience of parenting four children, fostering four others, and being grandparents of six grandchildren. Outside of that, Molly has been active in voluntary organisations with families living in poverty, and currently serves on the Glasgow Children's Panel, believing that *'if children don't get what they deserve, they become adults whom no society deserves, and who no individual deserves to be'* (Rosalind Miles, *The Children We Deserve*). John is a retired Church of Scotland minister, and was Leader of the Iona Community in the 1980s. Both of us served on the staff of Iona Abbey in the early 1970s, and we are both still members of the Iona Community.

Places: Iona Abbey Resident Group: Good community within which to see children grow in relationship to young adults; Iona the island: Child-friendly place for family holidays, which are such important times for developing holistic relationships between parents and children; Forsay caravan site, near Lochailort, Inverness-shire: Family caravan based there since 1980 – a safe place for us all, either together or separately.

Ruth Harvey lives in Cumbria with Nick and their three daughters, where she is a member of the Religious Society of Friends and a minister in the Church of Scotland. She works as the Ecumenical Development Officer for Churches Together in Cumbria, and as a Congregational Facilitator for the Church of Scotland in Annandale and Eskdale. She has been a member of the Iona Community since 1994.

Bridget Hewitt lives in Northumberland where, as well as writing, she is involved in running groups with teenagers and adults which encourage an open spiritual outlook. She is a wife, mother, daughter: the interplay of each of these roles, alongside her own space, is the warp and weft of her life.

Liane Kensett: I enjoy the richness of my family and community, and my work as a Forest School practitioner. When I have 'me time' I like to read, swim and make things.

Places: Same as Ros

Ken Lawson: Born in Morocco, lived in manses for most of my life. Married Mary and together we had three sons and now have seven grandchildren. Ministered in parishes in Paisley and Cumbernauld and learned much about myself and why I am the way I am. I was appointed an Adult Advisor in the Department of

Education of the Church of Scotland and later as a staff member of the Scottish Churches Open College. My responsibility was to train local tutors in the areas of pastoral care, listening skills, small groups and spirituality. The last was partly carried out as a member of the team in a Jesuit retreat house.

During my parish ministry, as a result of the breakdown of my immature belief, and following therapy and support, I became interested in counselling as a form of ministry. I later trained and practised as a counsellor in church and community.

I have been retired for over twelve years, thus enjoying space and time spent in a number of pursuits: pottering and pottery, gardening, reading, photography and sampling an occasional single malt. Above all, I am spending more time with the family who, in three generations, have taught me so much (when I have taken the time to listen, see and reflect).

Places: Anywhere in the countryside: the children taught me something of wonder and awareness. Talking with my grandchildren: I learn to come down off my high horse and rediscover my inner child.

Flo MacIntyre: Cumbrian born and bred. Went into social work after St Andrew's University but eventually taught outdoor pursuits. Was full-time wife and mother for 20 years, and now leading, or cooking for, long-distance walks.

Places: Iona: slow pace of life, the Abbey at the heart of every holiday, religion absorbed pleasurably; Cumbria: child-sized hills, old Cumbrian worthies of my mother's generation who taught my girls lots; Strathaven Park: a brilliant place to go on a nice day, well-kept and lots of uncommercial things for children to do.

Murdoch MacKenzie has been a member of the Iona Community since 1965, worked for twelve years in India with his wife, Anne, has three grown-up children and two grandchildren. He has worked ecumenically all his life, was Ecumenical Moderator in Milton Keynes and more recently Research Advisor at the World Council of Churches Ecumenical Institute in Bossey, Switzerland. He is now retired and lives in Argyll.

David McNeish worked as a hospital doctor, worship musician and campaigner for the Citizens Advice Bureaux, before admitting defeat and training as a Church of Scotland minister. A member of the Iona Community, he lives in South Queensferry with his wife, Sally, and three young children.

Peter Millar is a minister of the Church of Scotland, a well-known writer and campaigner and a former Warden of Iona Abbey. With his late wife, Dorothy, he worked in India for many years. The Dorothy Millar Trust, which he started, helps to support many small projects in different countries. His home is in Edinburgh.

Lucie Miller: Born in former Czechoslovakia to a minister, my childhood was filled with adventures of 'illegal' Christian activities, like children's Bible studies in the manse, summer canoe trips, scout camps and weekends with other Christian youths. Thanks to the oppression of the regime, my sense of belonging to the church has always been very strong, but was in a way taken for granted until my family emigrated to Scotland in 1985, where my father was invited to continue his work as a minister (which became impossible for him in Czechoslovakia). The period in Scotland, at the very beginning, was marked by a sense of a huge loss of something very special. Suddenly people around me in church on a Sunday morning did not seem to feel any special sense of belonging together, to a community that shared the same beliefs. This lasted for several years, until I learnt of the Iona Community and discovered that, yes, even abroad, there are people who feel that sharing time and experiences is fundamental to Christian faith.

Living in Scotland meant that I was allowed to study. I did my MA at Glasgow University in German and Czech, and then spent three years in Heidelberg, where I studied Education, which I then continued at Jordanhill College back in Glasgow, before becoming a fully qualified teacher of Modern Languages. I have been able to collect all sorts of incredible experiences from working with children in quite difficult schools in West Lothian and later in Fife.

It was great to work on Iona for ten weeks in 1996 and to meet Alan, to whom I have been married for sixteen years now and with whom I have the privilege of sharing our Christian life in different settings (parishes in Scotland, Paris), our membership of the Iona Community and not least our two sons, Jacob and Barnabas.

Places: Hospitals when Alan was being treated for leukaemia. Isle of Iona: We have had as a family some marvellous weeks on the island and have always felt renewed and encouraged in our faith. It was also wonderful to watch how children love the sense of belonging and sharing in such an intense environment, where people end up sharing a whole lot more than they are willing to at first. Churches/home: Our lives in a manse and in a church give us a huge variety of encounters with all sorts of people. They are all very special and never leave our lives untouched. Our open door is a witness to what we believe a Christian community should be about.

Yvonne Morland: What I think is really important is to encounter children as their own unique selves without imposing one's own agenda. Children often experience themselves and the world in a more integrated way than adults, responding with all their senses together, so when they are loved and supported it penetrates their understanding deeply. Sadly, when they are wounded or rejected their hurt is similarly deep. God bless all children and the child in each one of us.

Ellen Moxley: Born Nanjing, China, 1935, father Chinese, mother US-er. Moxley is stepfather's name. Naturalised Scottish, 1980. Worked in Vietnamese orphanage 1972–1974 (where I met Helen Steven). We ran Peace House 1987–1999. Active in Trident Ploughshares.

Places: The orphanage in Vietnam: total abandonment of beautiful young lives. Ochil Tower School (Steiner school): helping children to understand what is beautiful. Peace House: gave all three of us an experience of openness and acceptance.

Lis Mullen: Mother, wife, daughter, sister, mother-in-law, soon-to-be grandma, friend and Christian minister, and any time left for me is enjoyed by walking the fells, cooking, gardening or reading novels.

Places: Our tent – wherever it is pitched: holidays and fun together; New Zealand: a seven-month stay when sons were able to attend a different school increased their confidence, knowledge and experience; hospital bedsides: time to talk, reflect, learn, fear, pray together.

Bryan Owen is a former schoolteacher and Episcopalian priest who now writes full time. He has taught in the developing world and he has worked with the families of asylum seekers in Glasgow as well as serving on East Dunbartonshire's Education Committee. Currently he is volunteering with a nursing project in Dhaka, Bangladesh. His first book of poetry, *Blue Daffodils*, was published in 2007, followed by *Kokopelli's Dance* in 2010. His CD of poetry, *A Gentle Sprinkling of Stars*, was released in 2009.

Places: Over the years Bryan has been involved in projects helping Down's Syndrome children in Poland, street children in India, supporting a school in The Gambia, and he is currently volunteering at a College of Nursing in Dhaka, Bangladesh. In many parts of the world children are born into a poverty from which they find it almost impossible to escape. How do we in the West help children in such situations without being patronising or imperialistic? The truth is that we cannot separate children from their families or their culture. Our approach has to be inclusive.

Katy Owen is a member of the Iona Community; married to Bryan and mother of Catriona who has Down's Syndrome and Stuart who has lots of patience.

Places: Wallace Monument, Stirling: climbing the spiral stair and reaching the top, where Catriona exclaimed, 'Mummy, my legs are shakeling!' (but she did it!). Mountains are always significant, Ben Nevis in particular: they help get everything in perspective, and give us a sense of 'yes we can!'. Iona: Catriona 'disappeared', and was found in the shop trying to buy an ice cream. Everyone went looking for her – I felt then the value of community; love and caring.

Neil Paynter has been a farm labourer, a fruit-picker, a security guard (reluctantly), a bookseller, a hospital cleaner, a stand-up comedian, a worker in homeless shelters, a nurse's aide, a mental health worker, an editor …

Places: For me, it's more about places where I was a child, and keeping that 'child' alive. I don't have children. Might have been nice, maybe. I've never ached for it. The ravine behind my childhood house in Toronto: fossils, wildflowers, creek, drainpipe, river, poison ivy, bees, picnics, friends, summer sunshine, deep grass: a place in my heart now. Working at the YMCA, teaching English as a Second Language to adults and children who had just come to Canada. Amazing people from Nicaragua, El Salvador, Vietnam. Stories of survival and deep spirit.

Brian Quail: Prisoner No. 7164. Quail, Brian Michael, religion R.C., born 24/03/1938, former principal teacher Latin, Greek, Russian, father of seven, grandfather to fifteen, member Pax Christi, Iona Community, Scottish CND, Scottish Socialist Party, Trident Ploughshares. Into Russian icons, wildflowers, curry, reggae, Gaelic, Ravi Shankar, poetry, Gregorian plainchant, beer, Orthodoxy, Georgian history, Russian church music, Bob Dylan, Dostoyevsky and Mozart.

Places: St Patrick's Church, Strathaven: I used to go there each Sunday with my family. It reminds me of those days before my marriage broke up, of my children, me, and my wife Mary being together as a lovely little universe in ourselves. My daughter Anna got married there. Millport: I used to go there as a child. It always seemed like heaven to me, and I took my own children there. My Uncle Josie has his name on a war memorial there. It is so peaceful and lovely – it still seems heaven-like to me. Strathaven Park: I used to take my children there before and after my marriage ended. It is full of memories and still a very painful place to visit.

Em Strang: Dougie and I were married in St Oran's Chapel on the isle of Iona, 1999. Dougie spent many years living and working on Iona, mostly as gardener at the St Columba Hotel. We got together when he was helping to run Camas on the isle of Mull, 1998. Both these places remain special to us. We have taken our daughters to visit them.

We divide our time between community work, income-earning (gardening and working for our homegrown collective, The People Centre) and spending time with our girls. I'm also currently studying (MPhil in Ecopoetry) and am working towards my first collection of poetry. Both Dougie and I are engaged in trying to respond creatively to climate change and biodiversity loss.

Suzanne Swanson, a mother of three grown children, works in St Paul, Minnesota as a psychologist specialising in pregnancy, postpartum and mothering. Her book *House of Music* was published by Laurel Poetry Collective in 2005. She has been published in many literary journals. Proceeds from her chapbook *What Other Worlds: Postpartum Poems* go to either Postpartum Support International or the Childbirth Collective.

Places: Crosby Farms Park, St Paul, Minnesota: A natural area on the Mississippi with trails we could reach in 10 minutes from our house – quieting, calming, exciting (the dragonfly! the heron!). Cobblestone Cabins, Tofte, Minnesota: Rustic cabins on the rugged north shore of Lake Superior. We'd spend a few days watching the water and the sky, letting time unfold, eating well, jumping in the frigid lake after a sauna, sleeping to the sound of waves. Boundary Waters Canoe Area (BWCA), northern Minnesota: Going either with children or without helps me shed a skin, or worry and busyness, opens me to what's right in front of me: the basics of physical sustenance, where to make camp, what to eat, how far to go; and beauty, great beauty.

Elizabeth Wild: I am a mother of four daughters and have been a mother for my entire adult life. I have worked for many years as a Clinical Psychologist with children and families in a range of situations, from living with medical conditions or learning disability to experiencing the challenges of life in areas of urban deprivation. I am currently training for ordained ministry in the Church of England, and am a Member of the Iona Community.

Places: Iona: When my younger children were asked recently for advice on good places to take small children, they said, 'Iona'. My eldest still remembers cart-wheeling down the aisle of the Abbey in a service. Borde Hill: We spent a lot of time in this beautiful garden when the girls were small. Our allotment: Another place of refuge and productivity to share with small and large girls – especially when the fruit is ripe.

Rachael Yates: I live in Portobello, Edinburgh, by the beach, with Andrew, Imogen and Flossy. I'm a member of the Iona Community. As well as being a mum, I spend my time learning to be an English teacher in Secondary schools. To relax I love lying in bed (asleep or awake – it's all good), playing piano, flute and singing, building sand castles, sledging (I've recently discovered), cooking and gazing at the sea.

Places: Iona: The beauty, the friendships formed, the demonstration of commu-nity, inclusiveness, play, creativity, music. Times on the beach with other fami-lies, and the conversations we've had. Worship which moves me. My church, St James the Less, Leith: Feeling part of a community, where it's not 'weird' to be Christian! Knowing that others are helping the girls in their spiritual journey, that it's a shared task. Friendships, laughter, food, connection, inspiration to keep me going from week to week. A place where I am valued, and people see all sides of me. My mum's house: This is a place where our family can flop, take time out, and find space to reconnect and enjoy simple pleasures. My grandma was very important to me, and taught me a lot about God in her care of us – the girls are learning the same from my mum!

Wild Goose Publications is part of the Iona Community:

- An ecumenical movement of men and women from different walks of life and different traditions in the Christian church
- Committed to the gospel of Jesus Christ, and to following where that leads, even into the unknown
- Engaged together, and with people of goodwill across the world, in acting, reflecting and praying for justice, peace and the integrity of creation
- Convinced that the inclusive community we seek must be embodied in the community we practise

Together with our staff, we are responsible for:

- Our islands residential centres of Iona Abbey, the MacLeod Centre on Iona, and Camas Adventure Centre on the Ross of Mull

and in Glasgow:

- The administration of the Community
- Our work with young people
- Our publishing house, Wild Goose Publications
- Our association in the revitalising of worship with the Wild Goose Resource Group

The Iona Community was founded in Glasgow in 1938 by George MacLeod, minister, visionary and prophetic witness for peace, in the context of the poverty and despair of the Depression. Its original task of rebuilding the monastic ruins of Iona Abbey became a sign of hopeful rebuilding of community in Scotland and beyond. Today, we are about 270 members, mostly in Britain, and about 1500 associate members, with over a thousand friends worldwide. Together and apart, 'we follow the light we have, and pray for more light'.

For information on the Iona Community contact:
The Iona Community, Fourth Floor, Savoy House, 140 Sauchiehall Street, Glasgow G2 3DH, UK. Phone: 0141 332 6343
e-mail: admin@iona.org.uk; web: www.iona.org.uk

For enquiries about visiting Iona, please contact:
Iona Abbey, Isle of Iona, Argyll PA76 6SN, UK. Phone: 01681 700404
e-mail: ionacomm@iona.org.uk